T0327897

LIFE
IS
A
VORTEX

Linda Loppa

SKIRA

VORTEX

curiosity / empathy / imagination
spaces / meetings / transformations
anger / courage / quality
memories / layers / taking time
tension / intuition / puzzle
transition / liquid hybrid society / identity
conversations / pavilions / bridges
chaos / critical awareness / curating
invisible messages / geometry / sharpness
non-linear thinking / laboratory / future

VISION

CIRCLES ARE ROUND... OR MAYBE NOT
STORIES BY LINDA LOPPA

So, you agree that life
is a vortex...
Now the question is,
what's your place in there?

You can deal with this book in a number of ways:
- navigate through Linda Loppa's personal story in which some of the most memorable events in contemporary art and fashion are layered with tributes to her significant people, places, and things;
- use it as 'a guide for understanding how creative people act and react';
- read it as a map;
- brain-pick from a major fashion catalyst;
- bake Linda's slogans into fortune cookies and draw one when experiencing a creative block (think Brian Eno and Peter Schmidt's *Oblique Strategies*);
- test her *ten rules for archiving and using memories* and see where this gets you, personally and professionally;
- try to figure out why the *Vortex* appears nowhere in Linda's texts, except for the title.

A clue to the last one is hidden right at the beginning of the book: 'One must stand outside the circle to see that it is round', says Salman Rushdie's character in the opening quote. Reverse this observation, and you'll spot the only place from which Linda Loppa could have written her book. It's *inside* the Vortex. And mind you, not anywhere inside, but straight in its core, where — as physics explains — *the velocity is greatest while the pressure is lowest*.

Which is probably the book's most transformative insight, especially for a reader who is a young professional in a design-related discipline — or in any creative field, for that matter. The one trying to find their place in today's world where the pace of life and the amount of pressure only seem to increase. In the 'age of content shock' where exponentially growing volumes of information have long surpassed the human capacity to consume it, how does one make a difference?

Linda Loppa describes the contemporary society as hybrid and liquid. It doesn't dictate any dominant style to follow but digests pretty anything; instead of a homogenous identity, it fans out a multiple choice of social and cultural cues; the state of flux is the source of both its strength and its vulnerability. 'Thanks to the liquid society we are hybrid, we are multiverse; we are a set of [...] possible universes comprising everything that exists such as space, time, matter, and energy... we are visible but simultaneously invisible; we are versatile, but also liquid. We are multi-, but also one', she says.

As a tutor and a mentor who trains her students for acting in this society, Linda teaches through conversation. She won't provide immediate answers, only provocative questions. She won't tell you whether *living in an exciting world* is 'good' or 'bad'. In search for answers, you will learn to pay attention. To look, listen, feel, notice. To make sense of things. To foster your empathy, curiosity, and sharpness. Before you know it, you'll be asking your own questions, and that's how your identity will start to develop — like a film that gets developed in analog photography, revealing the latent image.

But this will only be the first step, followed by the crucial one — the step from identity to vision. By then, you would have already identified your place in the Vortex. You'd have realised that the more you depend on the pressure of someone else's opinions, the further you are from the core of this Vortex — and from having a vision. Because, if you are not the core, then you are being funnelled.

It would take a major mental leap to recognise yourself as the axis of your own Vortex — but then your perspective of the liquid, hybrid, and exciting world would change radically. Here is a book about thinking and acting from just that place.

Anna Yudina

The next morning we drove on to Aix-en-Provence and the following day continued to Saint-Amour where we had a rest before the final stretch to Paris. We did this journey nine years ago, in the other direction, starting from Antwerp with our suitcases packed and stopping then too in Saint-Amour and Aix-en-Provence before arriving excited and motivated to start a new life in Florence! We discovered the beauty of Tuscany and its life-style; a dream that seemed the utmost experience for us to have. Nine years later the dream has partly come to an end. We now see the reality of the dream and have discovered the rawness of the country, poor in origin but rich thanks to their cultural history and their vibrant past. The dream became transparent, the detailing sharper, less romantic, thus more real-istic. Voices were harsher, the comments of taxi drivers were always less civil, more surly, the food less flavoursome. But strangely the day before leaving we saw Florence as in those early days again; beautiful and sunny, the Duomo in all its glory, shining against the brilliant blue sky, the 'Opera del Duomo' museum stunningly renovated, and even the food seemed better. Yet people need challenges and those challenges can translate into sorrowful acts, but that's the force, the drive to excel oneself. The drive that supports the daily job, the passion to implement ideas, the an-ger when criticizing others or seeing them make errors. This has to be the starting point for the new adventure, the next step, the fantasy, the dream. With each new dream your body and mind become one, with each new dream your mind is in full action and your brain is in overdrive. Both are in dialogue, discussing strategies and decision-making. They cannot escape the drama of existence and the reality of the dramatic situations we are living or seeing. Long-term visions are the stimulus for short-term decision-making. What is important is courage, because without courage time stands still, the dream does not come true, and slowly slowly it will turn into a nightmare.

I believe in my anger, because it can be the drive to make things move. It is not always a nice experience but when somebody steps on my toes I am at my best! I am sharper, more lucid and direct, I work better, thinking of the puzzle to piece together, to compose or re-compose and draw up new diagrams. They guide me in my thinking when I explain to others what they need to achieve with a new strategy and how to make the new challenges work for them.

Our first hotel room when we left Florence for Paris in Forte had the room number 16, the number of the arrondissement where we are going to live. The second room was in Aix-en-Provence and was number 8, the house number of our new apartment in Paris. The third hotel and room were the very same we stayed in when leaving Antwerp for Florence nine years ago. Before arriving in Saint-Amour, our last stop, we visited Vaison la Romaine, where much of the book *The Dream of Scipio* by Iain Pears is set. Dirk is now reading the book on his iPad in French in order to improve his knowledge of the language of Molière while living in Paris. I myself started to read the book in English on my iPad, but I am more familiar with the writing and reading of the language of Shakespeare, if I have to better understand the complexity of the three interwoven stories. Sometimes I continue reading it in Flemish; we have the book in our library and I can check the refinements I sometimes miss because I am not a native English speaker. Finally I finish reading the book on my iPad in the English authentic version. Avignon, Vaison la Romaine and Paris are the three cities where the lives of the three characters, Manlius Hippomanus, Olivier de Noyen and Julien Barneuve, unfold. Three highly complex stories of relationships with friends, masters or women. Three complex realities of religion and politics, in three different periods of history, namely during the fall of the Roman Empire, at the time of the plague and the decline of the pope in Avignon in the 14th century, and finally between the First and Second World War and the extermination of the Jews in the 20th century. Those are the three stories that form the common thread of the book. A man was passing by when we were admiring the ruins of the Roman city in Vaison la Romaine. He had a backpack and his step was more decisive than that of a tourist or a local inhabitant. He paused before the small church, approached the main wooden door, opened it and stepped inside; he made the sign of the cross with the holy water, then went to the front of the church and sat down in the second row. The sun came in and shone on him! There were only the three of us in the silent church. He closed his eyes and started to pray. For me he was the reincarnation of Olivier de Noyen, the poet and scholar.

While we were driving in the beautiful open landscape, I reflected on all those interwoven personal stories. History is full of coincidences, traumatic or not, joyful or not, dramatic or not. But it is you and only you who is the force who can make those coincidences happen; nobody can dictate your destiny, only you can do that.

We arrived in Paris fourteen days after the shooting of 221 young people, leaving hundreds of people traumatised by the terrorist attacks in the Bataclan and five other locations. But we decided not to give in. We even came to Paris the day the conference on climate change started and traffic was banned in the city. Even this didn't stop us. We walked to our new neighbourhood and we were happy! We did it!

"UGO RONDINONE: I ♡ JOHN GIORNO"
Palais de Tokyo, Paris 2016
i-phone Linda

TO DIRK

THE ENCHANTRESS OF FLORENCE
SALMAN RUSHDIE

Chapter 6
When the sword of the tongue is drawn.

The silence thickened like curdled milk. Akbar's face blackened. Then all of a sudden the storm passed, and the emperor began to laugh. He slapped Mogor dell'Amore on the back and nodded vigourously. 'Gentlemen, an outsider has taught us a great lesson'. 'One must stand outside the circle to see that it is round'.

Dirk was invited by the artist Dominique Stroobant to present a film he made on Carrara and the marble mines, entitled *Dietro i Sassi* to the 37th Venice Biennale at the Belgian Pavilion. Simultaneously, Dirk was commissioned by Belgian TV (BRT) to document on the 37th Biennale in Venice of 1976 'Environment/Participation/Cultural Structures' or 'Ambiente Arte'. This Biennale was a totally new Biennale in its concept and in its organisation; the reason of the changes lies in the '68 movement and the changes in vision based on discussion and understanding. Since '68 the message was to re-think the Biennale, make it less commercial asking a greater possibility of participation on the part of the viewer; the Central Pavilion became more international in scope, 'a feeling that art can move from its formal setting into its own "space"'. I spoke a little Italian, because of my Italian roots, and Dirk asked me to interview Michelangelo Pistoletto while we were painting with him the walls of a warehouse in pink at the ex cantieri navali on the Giudecca land end, named 'Silenzio Rosa'. I remember making a cotton dress for going to Venice. We had little money and thanks to the hippie movement it was fine to wear self-made hippy-style dresses. And we had obtained authorization to fly over the city of Venice in a military aeroplane. The documentary was a kind of Land-Art master study. My husband interviewed Joseph Beuys and Pierre Restany; we met with Richard Long in the Great Britain Pavilion, where he showed a work that many years later changed our way of living. In the Central Pavilion we discovered work by Jannis Kounellis… some horses standing in an empty space. What great moments we were living!

Timeline

Houses

Back in Antwerp, before being married, we were introduced to great architecture at the house of our good friends. We were spoiled because we were often invited to this house for parties and drinks. So, when we had to choose the furniture for our first apartment in Berchem, we bought modern furniture from Joe Colombo. Three years later we bought a small country house in Schilde, in the countryside near Antwerp. The ground was damp, but in our enthusiasm, we didn't see that. We converted the small cottage into a small villa; with the help of our parents and friends we were able to transform it into an attractive and interesting house and pay our mortgage. After nine years, we changed the interior, buying Le Corbusier chairs and we put concrete tiles on the floor but after all, we were not happy with the result. We sold it for (what we thought at the time) was a good price.

Art

Art Has Always Been the Trigger

Our way of living and thinking changed. One day when living in that country house, we met the art collector Anton Herbert and his wife Annick. She distributed the collection of France Andrevie and later of the Belgian designer Dirk Van Saene, and because of my shop in Quellinstraat I was interested to see the collection. The Herberts transformed a formal warehouse in a loft and when I entered the car park in Ghent I saw the writing of Laurence Wiener on the external wall of the warehouse: **MANY COLORED OBJECTS PLACED SIDE BY SIDE TO FORM A ROW OF MANY COLORED OBJECTS - LAURENCE WIENER** Inside I was captivated by a work of Richard Long forming a circle in a beautiful and perfect space. Here a Dan Flavin on the wall and there a Jannis Kounellis in different corners of other rooms. This was a way of living that I felt was close to our philosophy; and the couple was so inspiring! I immediately called Dirk and ordered him to jump into his car and come over to Ghent to see the house. That moment changed our lives! We immediately put the villa up for sale and we sold it quickly. With that money we wanted to buy a warehouse to transform into a loft! And so, we did. After searching for many months, we saw an advert saying: Warehouse for sale, 570m^2. We went to see it and it was actually three floors of 570m^2; a few days later we bought it. My parents were on holiday, it was the month of August; we were so convinced, but the warehouse was in a bad condition. You could see the pigeons and the sky above us! Many friends admired our courage… or were worried by our imagination and naivety. Who cares? It was the beginning of an amazing period in our life! When by chance I showed Wouter Hoste, a student of mine, the pictures of the warehouse we had just bought he said, well, my friend is an architect, why not talk to him. Good! I always like to work with young people and I invited him to my shop in Quellinstraat. Later he confessed that he parked his shabby old bicycle around the corner because he felt embarrassed with the great contrast to my fashion store. He had just graduated and had little experience, but this did not matter to Dirk and me.

Living in a 1,700 square metres space is a pretty extreme way of living. The loft...: the brief to the architect Kris Mys was very simple; put the staircase here, like Le Corbusier, from the basement to the second floor in one line to the sky, two chairs there, the industrial kitchen here; on the second floor the bathroom and the bedroom. In the middle of the building was an elevator for transporting goods, and there were those empty spaces where you could see down to the basement and up to the floor above. In fact this simplicity was easy and complex at the same time. Kris, our young architect, was silent, but I felt our choice was made. My husband and I met him a few times and one day he brought a mock-up of the building. Amazing! We started working immediately on the sheer emptiness of the place. We finally achieved the most minimal result possible and we lived in that space for ten years. We wrote on the wall 'Less is more'. There was nothing more, oh yes, a TV and a sofa in the corner and, behind a wall, a library and an office desk. This ascetic way of living was a fantastic experience. I miss it now. Living in a city with a port makes a difference. Warehouses are perfect houses. You have no limits, no previous conceptions of what a house should be, only a shelter for feeling at home and being protected. A façade 19 metres long and a depth of 30 metres, divided only by a wall and the staircase. What more could you want of a house than all concrete spaces, with light coming from the street or in from the roof. We started to work on the 'Loft'. We put in floor heating, we built a staircase in concrete, we made a bathroom in white tiles and because we couldn't afford expensive designer bathroom furniture — there was none that inspired us — so we decided to use garden fittings instead. The light in this space was unbelievable. At night with a full moon you could sit in our 570 square metres living room and dream away. Thanks to our friends Anton and Annick Herbert, we rented out the ground floor to the best conceptual art gallery run by Micheline Szwajcer. Her portfolio consisted of names such as On Kawara, Niele Toroni, Laurence Weiner, Dan Flavin and many others. Can you imagine that we had a Dan Flavin standing in a corner of our living room and a Carl André on the floor, provided by Micheline Szwajcer? We also had an exhibition of furniture by Dan Graham in our house... Artists, photographers, friends came often to have a drink. The highlights of conceptual art were lying on the floor or hanging on our walls! Some time ago, November 2014, we returned to Anton and Annick Herbert thanks to our Belgian friends in Florence. Anton and Annick started a foundation a few years ago. Their collection of conceptual art includes Carl Andre, Lawrence Wiener, Martin Kippenberger, Bruce Nauman and On Kawara to name just a few, and is the best collection of conceptual art in the world. Can you image living among those artists, not only because you bought them at the right moment, but because you realised their creativity and their significance in translating a vision into a work of art. We were never able to afford their works, although we knew them in their early career, but that was absolutely irrelevant because we had their works of art printed on our mind and body. We walk with Anton and Annick to a restaurant and it is impossible to describe the emotional impact of this short walk. We remembered the first moment we entered their house and saw their art collection; the most iconic pieces, the most impressive art that entirely expressed the moment we were living. In 1968, Annick and Anton had been impressed and influenced by the occupation of the Palais des Beaux-Arts in Brussels by the artist Marcel Broodthaers. The mental, cultural and political changes of '68 had a great impact on a whole generation. I was 20 years old but '68 was a liberation of the mind and a liberation from the old values that defined art. This complete freedom has shaped what we have become, an older generation that is up-to-date, contemporary and curious, an example for many generations to come.

PUZZLE

My daily work is putting the pieces of the puzzle together. Fragments
of ideas, linked to situations, people or locations. When the puzzle
is completed my work will be completed. So I hope I will never find
the last ten pieces of my one thousand-pieces puzzle. As a child
I was never interested in puzzles, they made me nervous. I could
never find the match and it was too time-consuming. I couldn't concentrate or sit still. I was not a very playful child. I had no toys, no
dolls or comics. I did not want them, I was quiet and serious. I made
houses under the table of the dining room, or I drew in my room, or
later listened to music on my Braun radio. I am an only child and I
was not unhappy with this situation although sometimes all the attention from my parents was too overwhelming and then I behaved
badly, rejecting their love. I feel sorry about that now and would like
to apologise to my parents who passed away. Of course they knew
that I felt special as an only child. It made me a loner, and so I was
able to play a more intriguing role in the group and in my little society
composed of classmates and friends. But back to the puzzle. It is
strange that the metaphor of the puzzle is my way of explaining why
my decisions or changes need time. It is because I have to search
for the right piece of the puzzle and the right moment to put the pieces together. I cannot follow the logic that the game requires. I need
chaos, disorder, error, discontent, anger, and doubt to find the path
to the final construction. Not always easy for the team around me,
because I am not always able to explain why I need more time. They
can read my body language, my attitude, my gaze. They can read in
my eyes if I am angry or happy, worried or relaxed. Marina Abramović
sat for three months in MoMa, New York, in a performance called
'The Artist is Present'. She sat in front of a person that changed
every three minutes and looked into that person's eyes. It changed
their lives; some cried, some closed their eyes because her gaze
was too intense. When she sat in front of Ulay, her once life companion, she cried and took his hands in hers. The puzzle was complete

SCARS

Our body has scars... you don't see them; they are inside. They are wounds that have healed but occasionally they move in our body and come back to life to remind you of a battle you had to fight and then recover from. It is not always easy living a life that is quite exposed. You develop scars because you do more than is necessary and therefore you expose yourself to danger, to fragility, to aggression, to jealousy. It has happened a few times in my life — I could not speak or react, I could not cry. I needed time, silence, to overcome the pain, like an animal licking his wounds. We need scars; a body without scars is an uninteresting body; one that never took risks, that has not been exposed to danger, or believes in the easy way. Changing small things in life or in your job is a great challenge, first because change must be explained and motivated and second because you cannot do it alone. You need a team to support and implement change. The mood of today is conservative because our increasingly money-oriented society makes survival difficult, and the thought of change frightening. Looking back, we can analyse how '68 changed both society and the dialogue and attitude between a generation of parents and children. Later, after the fall of the Berlin wall in '89 and the arrival of the worldwide web, the generation born around and after this date has been exposed to rapid change. Hans Ulrich Obrist created the '89plus project to capture this moment and to help understand this generation. We all have moments when we break through walls and therefore have scars on or in our body. You learn when you are offended or aggressed by someone. You learn to be humble, to understand that people are sometimes stupid or pretentious or simply afraid or neglected. So, take care of your body and take care of your scars; they are companions till the end of your life, part of an inner dialogue about good and bad, strong or weak, right or wrong. Then, though once enemies, they will, eventually, become your friends.

THE MIRROR / OF SOCIETY / LOOKING IN THE MIRROR / WE SEE / WE INVENT / WE CHEAT / I CHEAT / I REFLECT ON THE SOCIETY / I AM A PLAYER OF SO MANY IDEAS / THE SOCIAL CRITIC / THE MIRROR...

CHAOS AND DEPRESSION / CREATIVITY NEEDED / PLEASE / CHAOS AND FUN / FUN NEEDED / PLEASE / THE WORLD NEEDS TO BE SHAKEN / THE POSITIVE CHAOS...

DRAMA IS EXCITING / REVOLT IS REVOLUTION AND EVOLUTION / WE NEED DRAMA / WE WANT DRAMA / WE ARE THE REVOLUTION / WE CREATE...

WE NEED MORE FANTASY / WE NEED MORE DREAM / WE NEED / WE DON'T NEED / WE WANT SUCCESS / WE NEED TO BE SUCCESSFUL / WE CREATE OUR OWN FANTASY...

UMANIZE
NEW
RENAISSANCE
DANGER
SOCIAL
ENERGY
SOUL
NEW
NEW
DISPLACEMENT
NEW
CHAOS
END OF
CIVILASATION
HUMAN
(DIS)ORDER

he mayor of Kanazawa, Japan, visited Antwerp in 2003. He was convinced that the success of the fashion designers in Antwerp held the key for the success of the future Kanazawa Fashion City. He invited me to Kanazawa. I gave a lecture in the 21st Century Museum of Contemporary Art, about Antwerp and the designers and how a few protagonists can stimulate a whole movement. I met Matthew Barney there, sitting in a corner of the museum hall. He was installing his exhibition *Drawing Restraint 9*, a film project consisting of a feature-length film, large-scale sculptures photographs, drawings, and books. *Drawing Restraint 9* is an unconventional love story set in Japan with a soundtrack composed by Björk. Shinto religion, the tea ceremony, the history of whaling in the sea of Japan and the supplantation of blubber with refined petroleum for oil.

The film primarily takes place aboard the Japanese factory whaling vessel, the Nisshin Maru, *in the Sea of Japan, as it makes its annual journey to Antarctica. Two storylines occur simultaneously on the vessel: one on deck and one beneath. The narrative on deck involves the process of casting a 25-ton petroleum jelly sculpture (one of Barney's signature materials), which rivals the scale of a whale. Below deck, the two main characters participate as guests in a tea ceremony, where they are formally engaged after arriving on the ship as strangers. As the film progresses, the guests go through an emotional and physical transformation slowly transfiguring from land mammals into sea mammals, as they fall in love. The petroleum jelly sculpture simultaneously passes through changing states, from warm to cool, and from the architectural back to the primordial. The dual narratives, the sculptural and the romantic, come to reflect one another until the climactic point at which they become completely mutual.*

shook his hand, but said something stupid like... nice work, bravo, congratulations. But it was at the exhibition in Kassel at documenta IX in 1992 directed by Jan Hoet, our Belgian pride, that Dirk and I saw his first artwork in a car park. He was climbing shafts, running and climbing, while three Scots, wearing the tartan kilts and bagpipes of the Black Watch where running and pushing a training apparatus around the car park. We stood there watching and trying to understand such strange actions and bizarre narratives. Reviewing your aesthetics and your ethics is always a good exercise, breaking the rules, your rules and concepts that reflect an impulse for a new lifestyle.

In the text of the catalogue we discovered we could interpret the underground car park with shafts and towers leading upwards as a gigantic instrument set in the belly of the earth with these microscopic characters speeding through the organisms. Later in Kassel we saw the *Cremaster Cycle*, a series of five feature-length films, made over a period of eight years (1994–2002) and the art work was a great shock for us but also to the world of contemporary art. Matthew Barney showed new imagery, new themes, and new tensions, simultaneously with intriguing imagery, compelling and repellent contrasts, the attraction and repulsion of beauty and ugliness. It was impossible not to watch those images and not be attracted by them.

Meeting a Curator

Meeting Hans Ulrich Obrist

I am sitting in the office of Hans Ulrich Obrist. I am in the Serpentine Gallery, Hyde Park, London. The meeting is planned for 9:30 a.m. but as usual I am too early. It is quite interesting to sit in the office of a man you know by his reputation, his books, his slogans, his concepts, his interviews, his writing, his fame. It is a small office, full of books, and I recognise the man through his desk. It feels comfortable although it feels like an intrusion into his personal life and work. After 45 minutes and after reading a few articles on him in books and leaflets, I look across the park. It's grey outside, raining, men and women jogging, running, or walking their dogs. The taxi driver told me a person drowned last night in the lake in Hyde Park, and so it was filled with police on patrol... But a strange calm came over me. Finally, he enters the office and there we sit chatting as if we had known each other for many years. He knows my work and this makes me feel comfortable. He talks about friends we have in common like Maurizio Nannucci, an artist living in Florence, and Chris Dercon who a few years ago hosted an exhibition on Maison Martin Margiela in the museum Das Haus der Kunst in Munich. He takes the phone and calls Chris; he has some messages for him and then he passes the phone to me saying to Chris, here is a surprise, Linda Loppa is sitting in my office. *Hello Chris... we talked about you this morning at breakfast, with Geert Bruloot, a friend of mine...* then Hans Ulrich asks me... what new project are you working on? I start talking about designers and my concern for the boring and uninteresting field I work in. The laboratory idea, the project he curated in Antwerp in 1999 together with Barbara Verlinden helps us in our conversation. He believes fashion designers might come from other fields than fashion itself. They might be poets. He thinks poetry is the purest of all the arts. Art & fashion are both industries now and therefore are not delivering any creative output. It is Hans Ulrich that launches the idea of doing something together, one day. He believed in the project '89plus... maybe we can involve designers and organise marathon interviews in New York... he believes we have to interview people born after 1989, after the fall of the Berlin wall. Yes, ok, why not. I speak about the IFFTI conference, the International Foundation of Fashion Technology Institutes and the event I am organising to happen in 2015, an excuse to hold debates, talks and I discuss the 'Moments' we are hoping for. Then he speaks of Dirk Snauwaert of Antwerp, a curator. He calls him and places the phone between us so we are all in contact; he wants us to talk… this is a great experience. Unfortunately there is no answer. And now I begin to know Hans Ulrich Obrist better. He stands up because we are repeating what we said before and it is Monday morning. He wants to start working. 45 minutes of creative talking and thinking. We leave as friends and he says… I am so happy we finally met.

Meeting with the City of Antwerp

Antwerp is a distant dream. Now that I am travelling to Antwerp to be celebrated by the Friends of the Museum for Fine Arts, I have the feeling that I am going backwards in time. It is as if all those memories I pushed aside are coming back. And it's the sad memories that take over... of friends or parents who have passed away, of ending a job, a relationship, a friendship, or moments of being hurt. It is my body that reacts, not my brain. And unfortunately, I do not seem to be able to control this. It is like memories are resurfacing and shaking your consciousness, dragging you far from logic and sentiment. It is like being fractured and being out of control. Why are we not robots — ruled by logic. First it is the city itself that takes revenge. The city feels abandoned, and asks why I choose to live and work in another.

Was living in Antwerp no good anymore, and what more has Florence to offer? Is it the weather, is it because the museums are more interesting, or is it the people — are they kinder to you?

No, no... the reason is, I was tired and not stimulated by you, the city. I had consumed all your beauty and all your knowledge.

I understand, but running away was not a kind solution.

Yes, but my husband and I did have the right to go and we did it perfectly correctly. All the people on my teams were informed, nobody was left aside. I nominated directors where necessary so they could work well, stimulated by their new responsibility and freedom. I felt I was becoming an old lady, tired and bitter. You have to understand, city... it was absolutely time for a change. Can't you see how much I gave to you? It was time to give to another city, don't be jealous!

Ok, but eight years abroad without coming back to see me is a long time; now finally you are here.

am quite nervous to come back to you. We have both changed, we have different opinions and different attitudes; our friends are different — and we are much older. Our ambitions are more specific and sophisticated and we, my husband and I, we see you, the city, in a more critical way, more objectively, related to the broader world we live in. We feel you didn't changed much and therefore we are a bit disappointed. You gave me a lot, starting from the river, the Schelde, to your port, but frankly, the river is a bit dull without the boats passing by and it seems the port is suffering from the economic crisis. By the way, it is correct that we are happier in Florence, it has a more relaxed feeling, my husband is a very good cook, the sunsets are amazing and the wine is excellent, the city is beautiful and clean and quite elegant. Eating on the terrace with friends in the summer gives us a holiday feeling. I know that you cannot give us all this, but you have to admit the food in Belgium is a bit heavy. And all that beer! And finally, can you tell me what you have done recently to attract my attention? The MAS museum... Yes, I can see, it's quite an achievement, but content wise... I am not so convinced! It's better than a Zaha Hadid or a Frank Gehry museum, that is for sure, but don't you need some good curators? Curating is the word we use today to embrace vision and strategic thinking. You are lacking vision, my dear Antwerp! Politics are disappointing, culture is absent in the debate for a better economy and the need to improve the urban plan is an on-going problem. Remember we used to have the *welstand commissie* — a commission that advises the city council on environmental quality in Antwerp. Now, there are some great project on the table, but that bridge 'de Lange Wapper' will never be built, will it? 'Antwerp '93 cultural capital of Europe' was a great moment for you, remember. You came to the attention of all the international press and tourists came to see you in all your beauty. ...But let's not be so nostalgic, my old friend, let's try to look forward; what can I suggest to you, to bring back a certain energy and joy to your citizens? Let me think... I would re-activate the Art Biennale in the Middelheim Park. But be careful; when tourists arrive they will discover that there is a lack of good five-star hotels in Antwerp! Look at the Four Seasons hotel in Florence; I often go swimming there in the summer with my husband, or have lunch at the pool. I cannot imagine a similar luxury hotel in Antwerp. How can you attract tourists if your infrastructure is not up to standard? And then shopping… There was a time that a lot of mono-brand boutiques opened because you were hip. Those days are gone (I guess) and therefore you have to invent new reasons for attracting luxury tourism. And what about the diamond business... are you still an important trader for raw diamonds? No, the wealthiest Jewish traders moved with their businesses and money to Israel. The poor Jewish community remained and Indians took over, sending their money out of the country immediately after a good deal. Taxes were finally raised and there is no longer the openness and care for communities that there used to be. Banks in the Diamond Centre closed down and trade is reduced to the minimum. This is not good news, my friend, because when I had my shops 30 per cent of my turnover was due to the Jewish community. Now I understand why your shops are suffering. I see a lot of black holes in the city centre and it's like watching a sick person dying from cancer. The city is suffering and it is very visible. Europe in general is asleep; there is lack of ideas and the economic crisis has driven citizens everywhere to look to their future only on a daily basis with no chance of investing in their future and preventing them from taking risks or consuming luxury goods. I can understand, but if I were younger I would go and live in Shanghai, New York, Hong Kong, or London.

But let's get back to our discussion; can we agree that you need new energy? I have to congratulate you though on some great achievements like the central station! The best! Coming from Paris arriving directly in the central station is very impressive! The different levels of the train platforms give a magnificent appearance to the station and it's a prestigious project for you. Dear friend, I have to say that my speech at the ceremony in the city hall on Tuesday 27 November 2014 was dedicated to you; you gave a lot to me so that I would be able to give back to you. I am very proud of you and I will continue to be so, but I have to tell you that you must be careful not to lose your prestige. You must dare to criticise politics and speak out — banish this notion that things are out of control. You must not lose all your ability to produce ideas and creativity because the economy is in crisis. We have had crises before, such as the Gulf war in Kuwait. I had to close my shop because of that difficult moment. You cannot let it happen twice! Find some solutions to make Antwerp as it was before. Take care, I love you more than ever, but I feel that you are losing the beauty you once had. Linda

I am working in a sector based on numbers. I like numbers and they like me. In the creative process, numbers are enemies but later, if you find the key to using them, they become useful. You can use your numbers for communication, for events, for a better quality of life, for services and better equipment. The fashion industry is economy-based and with this vision of it a strategy is needed to turn your creative power into a successful business. During the creative process there is only you and your thinking; the absence of the customer is a paradise that inspires you to perform and is the greatest moment for the joy of creating an object or a vision. This complete absence of a commercial aspect is the greatest opportunity for designing the future; there is only the future, there is no past. This is the moment to cherish — the beginning of a new process. The problem of the field I work in is that there is no time for those precious moments where the non-existent consumer is unable to influence your decisions. Time overrules the creative process, and the designer is obliged to perform when not ready, or not able, to produce a new idea. 1,000 fashion weeks frenetically overact, convinced they can deliver new performers and new ideas. Unfortunately they are not doing so; they are only complicating our lives, making the business more and more complex and more and more middle market. With millions of people in the world longing for clothes designed by designers it is only efficient to bring the level down. Supported by concepts of sustainability or fast delivery systems, this business is creating numbers and making money. The negative effect is the bulimia it creates and the addiction to garments that are not even necessary and do not make our lives any more interesting. We are not hungry anymore; we eat too much. We should eat better, appreciate the taste more, taking more pleasure from the moment and respecting the ceremony of the napkin, the rituals and the candlelight that accompany the enjoyment of food. It is the same for fashion: can't we relax in this hectic numbers-based economy?

DESIGNERS BUILD A CAREER IN FOUR MONTHS / WE RUN / WE FIT DAILY / FITTING / RUNNING / FASTER AND FASTER / CREATING AND REJECTING / AND NOW / WE ENJOY...

DRAPE / CUT / PIN / FEEL / SEE / CHANGE / WALK / DECIDE / CHANGE / CORRECT / DESTROY / BEGIN / CONCLUDE / BREATHING...

FASTER / AND FASTER / WE ARE BECOMING SLOW / SLOWNESS IS ENRICHING / RICH WE ARE OR WE BECOME / THANKS TO FASTNESS...

PASSION / BUILDING A CAREER ON PASSION / SO MANY STORIES TO TELL / SO MANY NIGHTS / DAYS / MINUTES TO SPEAK OF / A PASSION FOR WORK / MORE AND MORE, NO STOP, NO ENDING...

NEVER WILL WE STOP / WE MUST GO ON...

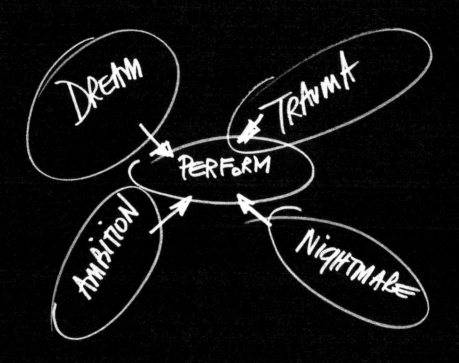

For MODE2001 LANDED GELAND, a project launched by the city of Antwerp and 'Antwerpen Open', I asked Walter Van Beirendonck if he would accept being the curator of the exhibitions. He accepted with joy and started working immediately. He conceived a great programme with several shows in the city: MUTILATE? – 2 WOMEN – EMOTIONS – RADICALS and a magazine called *N°A magazine*, the total underlined by colours on a big scale on facades becoming landmarks in the city of Antwerp. One of the projects imagined by Walter Van Beirendonck was an exhibition about two women he admired because of their passion for their work. The impact of their attitudes in fashion, but also in their graphic design, collaborations, statements, slogans, were for him the most important milestones in the history of fashion of the 20th century. One of the 'Two Women' was Coco Chanel, and her counterpart was Rei Kawakubo. We went to Paris to meet Rei in her showroom in Place Vendôme. Arriving at Place Vendôme I realised the strange link between the two women chosen by Walter; Coco Chanel lived in the hotel Ritz right opposite Rei's showroom and it seems to me that this is not a coincidence; two women with a strong character and vision choose one of the most famous squares of the world to live or to work. Can you imagine the thrill entering the showroom? The meeting was short and efficient. Walter asked Rei Kawakubo if she would join the MODE2001 LANDED GELAND project with eventually a show and an exhibition. Walter started the talk explaining that he wanted to provoke emotions, fascination, passion, authenticity and radical statements. She said *agreed*, I would like to do five shows. Each show will be in a different location, with a different number of invitations for each one, but with the same collection. We returned to Antwerp satisfied. I met Rei Kawakubo and her partner Adrian Joffe often on several occasions during the fashion weeks or events related to fashion; the pair is so charismatic that a real conversation is reduced to a nutshell, so much loaded by meaning that it remains in your personal memories and history books.

Paintings, Art and Art Memories; from Jos Mous to Zero

The workshop of Jos Mous was near the port and my father went there on Sunday morning to take drawing and painting lessons. I came to pick him up with my mother and we watched him draw (I can't really recall in detail but I assume it went like that). What I remember are Mous' black charcoal drawings of horses, strong and powerful, transporting wood, grain and other bales from the ships to land. Dark landscapes with grey skies; but paintings with colours, too; for example one painting that my father bought from Mous showed men painting a ship red as it lay in the dry docks. It seemed an enormous painting, though later I realised it was not that big. I have some charcoal portraits of my grandfather and grandmother from the 'Mous period' in my father's life. After his Sunday drawing lessons, my father took me to the Royal Museum of Fine Arts in Antwerp, in the south of the city, and we looked at paintings by Constant Permeke, Frans Hals, Antoon van Dyck and of course Pieter Paul Rubens. We didn't talk much, I think… we were fascinated by the compositions, the strength of the black and white drawings, the techniques painters were using and the stories they were telling. In the section of 'The Modernists' Permeke, the most Flemish of them all, drew in charcoal, powerful figures of people, poor rural people, but so complete within the frame and in their landscape. Looking at a drawing by Permeke I discovered the two-dimensionality of paper and the brutal, essential form of a body.

The passion of the drawing and calligraphy initiated itself when looking at the artist Pierre Alechinsky. I discovered that writing and drawing on the floor gives you a better view of a painting as your body is leaning over the artwork. When I look at Alechinsky I now understand why my father was so fond of his work. Alechinsky's storytelling, writing and designing take possession of the paper and a painting appears with colours, snakes, faces, circles, birds, trees and black lines forming a tableau that tells a story unknown to himself because it results from improvisation and physical en-

...rgy. Calligraphy is the key element of the body action of Alechinsky. He was surely inspired by the Japanese art of calligraphy but appropriated all the skills in a very personal language. Nowadays I realise why I observe and judge, the lay-out of a page or the strength of an image, by putting it on the floor.

Reflecting on my childhood I realise that my interest in art and art movements started in 1959 (at the age of 11) when a contemporary art exhibition held in 'the Hessenhuis', a warehouse in Antwerp near the port, created a big fuss. The Zero Group showed the work of artists who did not use paint. Fascinated, I looked at the work of artists like Lucio Fontana, Günther Uecker, Walter Leblanc, Jean Tinguely, Jesús-Rafael Soto, Paul Van Hoeydonck, Otto Piene and others who made art from poor or unusual materials, but very significant in expression. I found it interesting how artists could form a group and become a movement. Artists from France, Venezuela, Japan, Switzerland, the Netherlands, Germany and Belgium came together to express what they call a new beginning. But it is a fact that Zero was the start of a new way to look at Art. Can you imagine that the title *Motion in Vision – Vision in Motion* was launched in 1959 in Antwerp and that this exhibition was the start of their international breakthrough? And for sure my own breakthrough came when I was fifteen years old and entered the Royal Academy of Fine Arts where I could draw the nude guided by great teachers, artists in body and soul!

The frontier between the act of creating and the act of selling is not well defined. Confusion often starts with a societal shift. Over-consumption leads to over-acting and over-acting to over-designing or over-selling. This phenomenon leads to fast ideas, fast acquisitions and immediate indigestion. Stop mediocrity! Research and motivate emotional consumerism! Summer is sold in winter, haute couture is modern and designs everyday wear, men's wear is the new women's wear, and pre-collections are selling more than the show collections. Designers are not the stars of the project or of the idea — brand managers, production managers, communication managers, event managers, retail and shop managers are just as important. Maybe we don't need the designers anymore. The discussion is open; the designer has no time to design and therefore has no ideas. Menswear, women's wear, special projects, haute couture and pre-collections are designed in a few weeks. Managers come and go, designers come and go; they have nervous breakdowns, or go on to be paid more in the next company, or take a sabbatical to think… if there is time to think. What is there to think about? Will the speed of our everyday consumer society ever be ready to slow down? No, is the answer. We cannot turn back the clock. And it is better like that. Time is relative and after all we can decide not to buy a garment for a month or two. Do we do so? No.

Fathers are the mothers of today; they feed their three-week-old babies waiting for a flight at the airport or visiting a city to see its attractions. There is no time to relax and the baby is smiling. He will get used to the travelling because he is to become the global citizen of today, a citizen living and working for a few years in Shanghai, Rome, New York or Adelaide; the globe is a new challenge because we are connected with so many people and friends. We want to know them better or at least try to understand their culture or language. They will speak at least ten or fifteen languages because already I speak four. Confusion is chaos and chaos means a new beginning.

For a new beginning we need to redefine our values, or needs, o internal driving force. We cannot rely on others to show us the path We can find values in education and in our *sensei*, but the truth lies in ourselves regardless our age and origins, whatever the language the religion or the ambition we have in our job, in our marriage in our way of life or style of dress. Political situations are creating ground for wars; the human being seems not to learn from the pas because we continue to kill each other for a piece of land or a re ligious conviction. We are confused because there is freedom and freedom is frightening. But let's be positive… we live in a very excit ing world; we can write and speak to each other anywhere thanks to the Internet and we can become better informed, and if we use this information well we become richer in mind and thought. Creativity and the spread of creativity will be in the water we drink and the food we eat, the blogs we read or the implant we have in our arm o just the ink of the tattoo. The barometer of success will be redefined and the creative idea will be analysed by all the parameters of suc cess even before being born. There will be no failure or error, there will be no unreasonable action or trauma and the world will become a new world. We can buy it all, whether it is an object or an idea because we live in a world of consumption.

During the Renaissance, artists worked for their master or mae cenas, not searching for personal aggrandisement! Are designers working in the spirit of the Renaissance? Is the 'maecenas' more important than the artist? If that is the case, designers are less im portant than the product they make. The cult of the genius or sta is fading away — gone. It was quite romantic to think about the designer as a genius, a dreamer who gives us a dream and through wearing his clothes we too can become sublime. Identification with the artist, the idea behind his work of art or his expression o the idea is absolute, and wearing designer garments means identification with his tribe. If we lose this dream do we become anonymous? Are we obliged to have a greater, a stronger, identity in order to be recognised? What is the substitute for the fetish object they offered to us?

TEARS

I am known for being hard, tough, having a shield around me; they once called me 'The Warrior'. There is war and sorrow but my fight is different; it's a fight for quality and critical awareness. Tears are more sincere than words. Winning a challenge that required energy, a lot of strategy, alienation, uncertainty or fear brings an overwhelming joy that explodes in your body and mind. I cannot always hide my emotions; when students are leaving and I give a graduation speech it can happen that I have tears in my eyes or that my voice is trembling; when I give a promotion to a member of the team, I might feel tears welling up. Tears come easily, more easily than words. Can the reason for tears be scientifically explained? Giving a speech is an exhausting activity because your body and mind have to be concentrated, sharply tuned to express and communicate ideas and meanings.

POINT A FINGER IN ONE DIRECTION / WE ARE NOT USED TO GO THE OTHER WAY / THE GREEN MIGHT BE GREENER BUT WE ARE AFRAID / WE FOLLOW / WE ARE FOLLOWERS...

WE IMITATE OURSELVES / WE COPY AND PASTE OUR BRAIN / WE CAN ESCAPE / IT'S NEVER TOO LATE / IT'S ALWAYS TOO LATE / WE RUN AND WE EMBRACE TIME / WE ARE TIMELESS / ARE WE...

WE ARE EMBRACING / ITS UNCERTAINTIES / ITS CHANGING ATTITUDES / I FEEL CAPTURED BY THE EMBRACE / I CANNOT RUN AWAY / I HAVE TO LOOK, TO SEE / LOOKING IS SEEING...

TIME MUST BE TIMELESS / FASHION IS RELATED TO TIME / TIMELESSNESS IS BORN OUT OF FRUSTRATION / FRUSTRATION IS TO CONSUME...

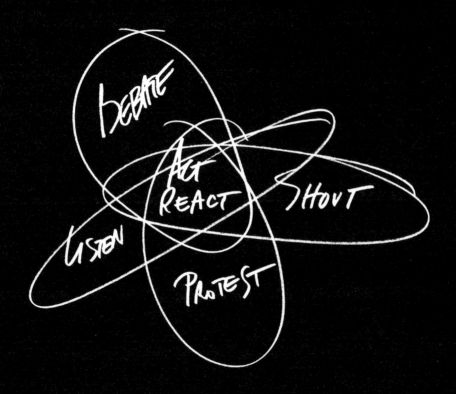

Alzheimer killed her, in fact her heart stayed alive for a long time, after her mind left her. Why? Because her heart was the most important part of her body; she was patient, humble, kind, fragile, everything a heart can bear. Her sickness also killed my father. But that's how he wanted it. A kind of guilt came over him the minute she became ill. They had a difficult life, a story of true love and partnership, but a life I feel they would have organised differently today, probably with more strategy, less responsibility, more natural and less stressful. Who to blame? The war? Probably yes. It was not an easy choice to marry during the war: he was very young, 18, and she more experienced — 22. She travelled to England to study, she had become an orphan at 12, inherited her parents legacy at 18 and was able to travel to Morocco with a companionable niece, both attractive young ladies, independent and always in good humour. And then suddenly one day at the RUA tennis club founded by the Royal Union des Anciens élèves de Mallones a young fellow came in, tall, black hair, tanned, handsome, Italian by the way! What on earth did she see in the guy? Well, look at the pictures and you have the answer! All the girls of the tennis club fainted seeing him entering the club in his white tennis trousers like the famous player Fred Perry! She was not interested or impressed. Ah well, there you are — the rules of seduction are not always those we think they are. He was attracted probably by her independent attitude… so, not so Italian after all! But because of the war he was mature at 18, driving a car, organising the life of his father stressed by the First World War. My father avoided being sent to war because he was the only boy in the family and my mother probably felt quite well settled marrying into a nice family of sailors and hard workers but I guess she envisioned a life full of excitement with an exotic flavour because of his Italianism? Well, work was a very important part of her life; she did the numbers, the accounting, she was the one who knew what there was to spend and what wasn't, but my fa- ther was the nervous one, always afraid of an uncertain future, never really able to enjoy me, I suppose. There were other children too, one before me and one after me, but no one ever explained to me why I was an only child. Companionship and complicity is the key for marriage, but there were many other characters in this marriage. First my grandmother, tall blond Rubens posture and dominant, then my grandfather, shorter, slim elegant Italian and speaking French, and Flemish in a comic way with this Italian accent, more critical but a super good tailor! They lived in the house on the other side of the street. My father came home to eat and went back to work until late at night because the business was growing and of course this was good news. But she was really quite lonely. She started playing cards on Wednesdays, and in the afternoon she had a nap. I feel this loneliness also in me. I look like my mother, I have her body, her eyes, and sometimes this makes me feel sad. I often went to Kapellen, to the summerhouse my grandparents had bought, and my mother took me there for weekends when they started to have a more social life in the tennis club with parties and friends, having fun. The garden was of Italian inspiration with all kinds of trees and flowers, but especially Italian cypresses. I recall that it was not so strange for me as it was just part of our culture. I enjoyed these weekends well enough, sometimes bicycling with the children of the neighbourhood but mostly sitting among the apple trees reading.

When my grandmother passed away I was alone with my grandfather and he spoke about the First World War. He had been a soldier for seven years and his stories about the Abyssinian war are still in my memories. He was scared and not so brave, he said, but he came home alive well, to Antwerp that is, captured and dying from tuberculosis and there she was his nurse blond, good looking, nice breasts right out of a Rubens painting, and she took care of him! But at the open fire in Kapellen we ate *polenta* or *gnocchi* in the winter, made by my grandmother who was a great cook, or we grilled *castagne* (chestnuts) in a special pan. I was destined to become Italian or at least to marry one! Destiny decided differently and this is good because destiny must always be followed. We were a nice family, different in a sense as we were a mix of cultural attachments, me with my black hair, blue eyes and a little dose of Italian blood in my veins, my father tall powerful, with strong opinions and my mother sweet, smart but silent and smiling. Are families today closer? Do they talk more often about their relationships, their common future, their dreams or despair? The gap between generations will always exist. I grew up as a difficult and different child I guess. At the tennis club I often sat apart in a kind of separate room; I would wear a black high-necked sweater and existentialism was my companion. My mother loved me dearly but she never said that to me; it was not done, I believe, and maybe she suffered from the absence of her mother who left her alone at twelve. Why did we never speak about this absence and the emptiness it left and why did we not compensate for it by hugging or hearing nice stories about her youth? I still have letters from her time at her English high school and I will read them again, but not now. When I married, thanks to my husband I joined a different family, more conservative, seemingly more family-oriented, and more gentle, less stressed. I had a good time spending Sundays in this new family, listening to their stories that were very different to mine.

My vision of architecture and art was based on my visits to churches, temples, convents and cathedrals. First came 'my' cathedral in Antwerp, where I could admire 'my' Rubens! Then of course all the churches I visited with my parents during our Italian holidays (my grandfather was Italian and so we came to Italy every year in August to visit some of the family in the mountains around Lecco and Lake Como). My favourites were, and still are, the church of San Miniato al Monte in Florence, the tomb or Mausoleo of Galla Placidia in Ravenna and the Byzantine mosaics of Sant'Apollinare in Classe, the paintings by Giotto in the basilica of Assisi, the temples and houses in Kyoto and in Singapore, and the baroque 'Carolus Borromeus' church in Antwerp. The spirituality of architectural buildings does reflect on our limited stay in this world. Ports and the greatness of their docks give you the feeling of being part of something bigger than just this place and this life. I learned much about appreciating this spirituality without being baptised or educated religiously. This freedom from purely formal religious boundaries made me a more complete spiritual person. Later, when I discovered the work of Bill Viola, I felt he captured this kind of spirituality in his work that refers to Fra Angelico and the frescoes in Florence.

Architecture

Fashion

From 1967 to 1971 I studied fashion design at the Royal Academy of Fine Arts in Antwerp. I wore hippie clothes; second-hand vintage, and I made my hot pants in neoprene. My first plastic vinyl boots were very sexy! My make-up was Twiggy-inspired; false eyelashes, freckles, eyeliner and a short hair cut. The film *Bonnie and Clyde* inspired me to wear a long skirt over my mini skirts or hot pants; my final-year collection was, on the contrary, quite classic. I was inspired by Italian style and Italian elegance. Valentino was my idol! Can you imagine that now? Well, yes, I had my weaknesses. This love for Italian style came from my Italian roots of course and as I understood later was also because of the Italian tailoring techniques my father and grandfather used for making those extremely elegant men's suits. When I opened my women's wear shop in 1979, I introduced Gianni Versace and Genny to Antwerp. At the end of the 1970s Italian fashion was modern, beautifully made and super luxurious. I fell in love with the Versace shop in Via Sant'Andrea in Milan, which was designed with grey tiles of 'pietra serena', and thought of it when I started to design my shop in Quellinstraat. The shop was completely decorated with 50 x 50 tiles in 'Blanc de Bierges', a stone that is found in Belgium. The very minimal architecture was a shock for Antwerp, but the shop became a great 'salon' where students, clients, friends came to chat and to show their work or just dropped in to say hello.

Huidevettersstraat

When the lease of my shop in Quellinstraat expired I could have closed my retail business. But I still had great ideas and something to say about the shopping experience. One day I stopped my car in Huidevettersstraat, one of the main shopping streets, and looked around me. I noticed an announcement for a lease on a first floor on a corner of the street, a good location, strategically interesting, above an electronics shop. The space was terrible but the lease was affordable. When I visited the property I discovered that my future clients would have to go through the shop in the basement to get to my store... well, this was a problem. But next to the shop there was another — empty — house. I asked the owner of the property if I could use it to construct the entrance to my shop and he accepted! Did he realise I was about to demolish all the floors and that I was going to construct an iron staircase right in that demolished house? The idea came from my young architect Kris Mys! I still remember looking into the depths and seeing the empty gap where the stairs would be built! How could we do this? By being courageous and by knowing this was a great architectural achievement! And it worked! We were in all the architectural magazines and all my clients came to see this innovative idea. The ceiling was a bit boring and so I asked my student Wouter Hoste to draw fragments of Michelangelo Buonarroti's paintings in the Vatican Chapels on the ceiling. As a joke we decided to dress god the father and other figures in Jean Paul Gaultier garments. So, god the father was wearing tiger print shorts, while the beautiful women on the ceiling surrounding him were in corsets. A theatrical scenography workshop named 'Ercola' painted the scene on paper canvasses, which we later glued onto the ceiling! The changing rooms for my customers were inspired by the 'pissotoirs' of the JPG shop in Paris. Hanging on one long rack were the garments I proposed to my clientele from the collections of famous designers such as JPG, Romeo Gigli, Helmut Lang and Comme des Garcons.

Architecture

MODENATIE

MODENATIE became the home for fashion in Antwerp. The building extended over 11,000 square metres which we divided into different functions; the Academy of Fine Art, Fashion Department of Education, the MoMu/ModeMuseum where the 19th-century collections of Vrieselhof were archived and where an innovative programme of exhibitions for fashion and clothing was launched. The Flanders Fashion Institute for supporting young talent and a bookstore were on the ground floor, and there was a space for various activities and finally — for pleasure — a restaurant. One day I met Josée Van Hée, an architect from Ghent, quite unknown but strong in the purity of form, in managing spaces, and yet practical and good at thinking big! We had a central, 19th-century building with a great staircase and a great façade and a smaller modern '60s annex in concrete with lower ceilings. Josée Van Hée did miracles! Of course we knew that the archives didn't need light, so the smaller concrete building was perfect. We also knew that the students who would come from all over the world to study fashion needed a top floor, looking across to the river Schelde and Antwerp Cathedral as well! We knew there was a good bookstore from Ghent, Copyright, whose owners wanted to open a shop in Antwerp, and we knew a restaurant would be a great opportunity to bring in the kind of entertainment and people we wanted. For the Fashion Museum I needed an open space, a good light installation, shutters we could open or close, and a system to provide a constant temperature when showing our archive pieces following the ICOM regulations. We also created a small gallery and an educational space for children's workshops. It all worked quite well. Finance came from the city of Antwerp (building), the Province of Antwerp (MoMu), the Hogeschool Antwerpen (Academy of Fine Arts), the Ministry of Economic Affairs (Flanders Fashion Institute) and private partners (recruited by the Chamber of Commerce). I will not go into the details of how complex the project was in this respect, but we managed to create this amazing project, opening in 2002.

Loft 12-14, Antwerp
Photograph by Tony Le Duc

met Martin several times at the beginning of his student career and late as a designer. The first time, I recall, was when he was a student on the Fashion Design course at the Royal Academy of Fine Arts in Antwerp. met the fourth year students as a guest lecturer, invited by Mary Prijot my former head of department. Before graduating, in my fourth year, she recommended me for a job at the raincoat manufacturer Bartsons. I had some experience in retail and manufacturing thanks to my father's shop n menswear. At Bartsons I had to prepare the collections, prepare the presentation to the sales team, make technical drawings, follow sales and statistics, especially for the German and French markets, visit the clients n both countries, visit the Textiles Fair in Frankfurt and understand distribution. My experience in the company of Bartsons was interesting for the Antwerp Fashion Design students as Belgium was not known for designing collections but more for producing fabric and production for others was sitting in a small classroom, probably talking about how to make a collection plan, or about distribution and design from buttonholes to colour cards. Martin was one of the students; I am not sure if my lessons were interesting. I was young and ambitious, and not only my experiences at Bartsons, but also accompanying my father to Paris buying for his menswear shop in Antwerp at the Porte de Versailles and the SEHM fair gave me a lot of information about the business side of fashion. I was no so attracted to become a designer and this must have been the reason to my teacher for pushing me in the direction of what I later became, a fashion critic.

Later, after he graduated I met Martin in Milan. He desperately wanted to oin the design studio of Giorgio Armani and was living in the apartment of Phara Van den Broeck, one of the first students who had graduated from the Academy in Antwerp. She was our pride for the school because working as a designer in Milan for Gianni Versace. I was often in Milan as a buyer for my men's and women's wear shops, and so we would go to have dinner together in a *trattoria* or partying in a disco at night with Sara and Martin!

Martin moved to Paris after presenting a beautiful and inspiring collection at the 'Golden Spindle' contest in 1981 in Brussels. This contest opened the doors for a group of young designers inspired by this new movement coming from Antwerp. His collection, inspired by the uniforms worn by doctors and nurses, was a start for a long and interesting career. After the contest, attracted by the energy of Paris' new creativity without borders, Martin joined the designer team of Jean Paul Gaultier. I recognised immediately the raincoats, the jackets and the classics designed or touched by Martin. Their tailoring, the positioning of the pockets, sleeves conceived and perfectly designed, the colours of fabrics amazingly beautiful and contemporary were the signature of Martin's strong aesthetics. I met Martin much later by accident in the streets of Paris. He announced the launch of his own collection and I was so happy because I felt it was the right moment. I had my doubts when he talked about wanting a good price-quality balance, because Italy was expensive in prototyping and through my experiences with my own shops I knew the problems of deliveries and price settings. It was of course a success and I don't have to rewrite history. Martin, who decided not to give in to the media and easy success, was not the front figure representing his brand. He was not photographed, he did not appear in the press, he wanted the garments and not the person to be the centre of all the attention. We of course accepted his strategy, which seemed based on great reflections about the fashion system, about his future and about the position a designer can have in a company. The persons who surrounded him with their creativity filled his absence. The strongest presence was Jenny Meirens, his partner in the business. What a woman! She had style, authority, passion and could run the business based on low budgets and great ideas. Shows were amazing, press and buyers pushing to enter the spectacles, because of the never seen locations, models, make-up and styles. The visuals were so refreshing, the garments so well made, the sleeves making you feel like a princess, the fabrics and the production the best I ever saw. When Martin started to work for Hermès, the emotions were so intense! I remember entering the first floor of the Hermès store in 24, rue du Faubourg Saint-Honoré to see his first collection and having tears in my eyes. So much beauty, so much craftsmanship was hardly to cope with!

When one day the news spread Maison Martin Margiela was sold to Renzo Rosso, I understood and accepted the decision, but in my heart I felt the changes were inevitable. Was Martin going to continue to design? At first we felt secured because the news was positive, but soon Martin stepped out of the Renzo Rosso vision and the reasons were clear to us. Keeping your integrity for so many years to give up to commercial success and commercial strategies was not meant for Martin! We have been used for many years now to live without the Maison Martin Margiela label designed by Martin himself. Difficult, because the garments were fitting so well to my body and mind! Especially the classics, the trenches, the blazers, the trousers, the knitwear…

And then, after many years of absence… I was sitting in a corner behind a pillar of the church during the funeral of a mutual friend… he came to me and kissed me… I am Martin… I put my hands in his and we sat there for a long moment, in silence… and there came all the memories of a beautiful past… a moment never to forget.

RAW IS ALL THAT IS NOT CONSERVATIVE. RAW IS ESSENTIAL THINKING. RAW IS THE BASICS OF LIFE. RAW IS FINDING YOUR SELF. RAW IS NOT CONCEALING THINGS BUT EXPOSING THEM RAW IS LOOKING SOMEONE IN THE EYES WITHOUT FEAR. RAW IS SAYING THE TRUTH. RAW IS LOOKING IN THE MIRROR AND SEEING YOURSELF AS YOU ARE. RAW IS YOUR OWN NAKED BODY. RAW IS WRITING WHAT YOU WOULD NEVER SAY. RAW IS SHOUTING YOUR OPINION OUT LOUD. RAW IS WITNESSING DEATH. RAW IS AGING RAW IS NUDITY. RAW IS EXPOSURE. RAW IS POVERTY. RAW IS LYING TO OTHERS OUT OF FEAR. RAW IS WALKING IN THE PARK WITHOUT FEAR. RAW IS LIVING WITHOUT GRATITUDE. RAW IS THE WRITING ON CITY WALLS. RAW IS LIVING IN THE STREET RAW IS WRITING ON YOUR FACE. RAW IS WORKING AT NIGHT AND DREAMING DURING THE DAY. RAW IS TRAVELLING THE WORLD WITHOUT LIPSTICK. RAW IS WAR. RAW IS BURNING YOURSELF TO DEATH. RAW IS MAGNIFYING MICROSCOPIC INSECTS. RAW IS SEEING ANIMALS EATING EACH OTHER. RAW IS FIGHTING TO THE DEATH. RAW IS PICTURING SURVIVAL. RAW IS TRANSPLANTING YOUR FACE AND BODY. RAW IS RUNNING, RUNNING, RUNNING RAW IS ABSOLUTE LOVE. RAW IS A NEVER-ENDING GIVING. RAW IS BEING CRITICAL. RAW IS OPTIMISM IN A RAW WORLD. RAW IS GOING TO WAR AT 12. RAW IS THE FACT YOU KNOW THAT YOU ARE RIGHT BUT YOU CANNOT PROVE IT. RAW IS DREAMING A DREAM THAT SEEMS REAL BUT IS UNREAL. RAW IS DOOMED TO HAVE THE LAST WORD. RAW IS FEELING THE END COMING. RAW IS LEAVING OUT YOUR BEST FRIEND. RAW IS HAVING SYMPATHY FOR THE LOSER. RAW IS MINIMALISM. RAW IS TO KNOW EVERYTHING ABOUT NOTHING. RAW IS BEING SAD OF HAPPINESS. RAW IS BOREDOM RAW IS BEING SPEECHLESS AND HAVING MUCH TO SAY

Avec le temps...
Avec le temps, va, tout s'en va
On oublie le visage et l'on oublie la voix
Le cœur, quand ça bat plus, c'est pas la peine d'aller
Chercher plus loin, faut laisser faire et c'est très bien
Avec le temps...
Avec le temps, va, tout s'en va
L'autre qu'on adorait, qu'on cherchait sous la pluie
L'autre qu'on devinait au détour d'un regard
Entre les mots, entre les lignes et sous le fard
D'un serment maquillé qui s'en va faire sa nuit
Avec le temps tout s'évanouit
Avec le temps...
Avec le temps, va, tout s'en va
Même les plus chouettes souvenirs ça t'as une de ces gueules
A la Galerie je farfouille dans les rayons de la mort
Le samedi soir quand la tendresse s'en va tout seule
Avec le temps...
Avec le temps, va, tout s'en va
L'autre à qui l'on croyait pour un rhume, pour un rien
L'autre à qui l'on donnait du vent et des bijoux
Pour qui l'on eût vendu son âme pour quelques sous
Devant quoi l'on se traînait comme traînent les chiens
Avec le temps, va, tout va bien
Avec le temps...
Avec le temps, va, tout s'en va
On oublie les passions et l'on oublie les voix
Qui vous disaient tout bas les mots des pauvres gens
Ne rentre pas trop tard, surtout ne prends pas froid
Avec le temps...
Avec le temps, va, tout s'en va
Et l'on se sent blanchi comme un cheval fourbu
Et l'on se sent glacé dans un lit de hasard
Et l'on se sent tout seul peut-être mais peinard
Et l'on se sent floué par les années perdues
Alors vraiment
Avec le temps on n'aime plus.

Avec le temps de Léo Ferré:
paroles écrites et chanson composée en 1969,
enregistrée en octobre 1970

OPINION

Reflections on the Train

Florence - Rome
to view the exhibition of Maurizio Nannucci at MAXXI

Streets became narrower and narrower, the sky darkened and the sun burned our skin as if we were in hell. Trees were torn out of the ground by a passing hurricane and the rain poured down so heavily that roofs fell in. Dante's inferno had come to life. Then the film crew blocked all the streets and we could hardly walk through the city of our dreams; they are enacting Dan Brown's theory that it's time to release a virus such as the plague because we are too many. Thousands of tourists take over the city blocking the streets like busy ants. Dante was right in saying that in hell we meet both our friends and our enemies. And then there is urban surgery! Arteries are sliced open to let the ants flow into the city faster!

To understand Florence you need to visit *When Dalí meets Dante* in Palazzo Medici Riccardi and read *The Enchantress of Florence* by Salman Rushdie and go and see the paintings of Piero di Cosimo exhibited in the Uffizi and watch Dan Brown's film *The Da Vinci Code*. Florence has all the ingredients for being decadent. The Medici stories are full of gossip and murders of passion, corruption and sexual abuse, sodomy or romantic excess. While building the Duomo and other marvellous historic buildings the city was 'under construction' for one hundred and fifty years and Florence was an open space where murders, jealousy, and a superlative form of creativity dominated life. Never again in history was there such a moment of concentrated beauty and passion. Amidst inventions, wars, exiles, the city also hosted the leaders of the Greek Orthodox and Catholic churches and their popes and patriarchs who influenced the art and fashion of Florence. Virgil, symbolising human reason, will show us the way through Hell and Purgatory!

My dear Florence... we all fall in love with you! Nobody can escape! The beauty of the landscape is breath-taking, the ugliness of the tourist invasion is disturbing; but it reflects today's society. We live in a very controversial world; on one hand I am looking for a 200-square metre apartment in Paris and at the same time hundreds of thousands of refugees are landing alive or dead on the shores of Italy and Greece. Homeless, without a job, they look for shelter, for work, with the hope of raising their children in a peaceful land. Is this too much to ask? Yet they are treated like animals; inferno is everywhere! I feel guilt but there is little I can do. I worked hard for this life, I feel I deserve the apartment we are looking for but when I see the news I experience an unbearable physical reaction that says sorry... sorry. Cities... you love them or hate them. They make you or break you. I definitely need the triangle Antwerp, Florence, Paris. I need the creativity and the conceptual part of Antwerp, the beauty and decadence of Florence and the elegance and richness of Paris. What was possible in Antwerp, starting from scratch, inventing it all without boundaries was like natural growing pains. Florence made it possible to jump into the future thanks to experience, a pragmatic approach and strategy, and Paris will give the peace needed to finish in beauty.

Five icons are embedded in my personality. Marcel Broodthaers, the poet and later artist, for his artwork the 'Mosselpot', for his cynical approach to 'Belgitudine' or 'la Belgitude' or 'Belgianness' for a country that lacks an identity. Tadao Ando, the architect and self-made man, for using concrete and light and for his minimalism and conceptual thinking. Leo Ferré, the song writer and poet for his nihilistic romantic soul, a rebel and anarchist to represent the rebel in me. Joseph Beuys, for his passion for life. The passion for survival, of experiencing every day created the *sensei* in me. Mies van der Rohe, for his amazing slogan 'less is more' symbolising life itself and the choices to make. Those are the metaphors that symbolise my life with all its memories, layers of experience, drama, love, sadness and joy. I am a lucky person because I do not forget the scars from hurt inflicted by ignorant people. In the end I thank them because they made me stronger. When I visited my great-grandmother in the Italian mountains of Bonacina

I saw her living in a house with floors made of sand and I suddenly realised that I was a lucky child. When I speak to friends who are in tears for the loss of a child I feel desperate because it's hard to imagine their pain, but I realise I am fortunate; when a son or daughter dies, I feel injustice because life is so beautiful; when I hear a friend took his or her own life because it was not what they expected, I feel sorrow, and I fear for future sorrows. When I attend a funeral I carry the weight of all the funerals I ever attended in my life and feel very lonely. When I feel the sadness of so many people suffering from loneliness I know I am lucky.

I look out of the window... Cities and their landscapes protect us; they are shelters for sorrow and pain; shelters for keeping history and knowledge alive. Shelters for intimacy where we can sit before the open fire and stare. While Antwerp symbolises experiment, Florence symbolises a dream, and Paris will stand for reflection.

Sift

Store (=tidy)
Serendipity (=untidy)
Personal archive: ten rules to archive your memories and how to use them.

1. Store the most valuable memories

2. Delete the most common memories after a while

3. Use the most valuable memories to understand when making future decisions

4. Never use your personal archive of memories for nostalgic purposes

5. Store the most valuable everyday emotions

6. Write down the memories that are important for the person you are today

7. Use the memories of others but take care not to appropriate them

8. Memories are layered; use the layers

9. Archives are precious; don't repeat them too often to friends and relatives, they will soon get bored!

10. Your archive is precious! Use it well.

1. Store the most valuable memories

Q: Not all your memories are valuable; but how do you know which will become valuable on a longer term and which not?
A: You cannot, it's your body and mind that will decide. If some memories disturb your body and mind you can delete them; but you have to wait till the memory itself is ready to disappear.

2. Delete the most common memories after a while

Q: How do you make this choice? What does 'common' mean and why are they not important?
A: Memories which are not important will fade away quickly; maybe it's you who is not giving any dedicated space to them. Your memory is limited and if they feel they are not welcome anymore they will understand, don't worry.

3. Use the most valuable memories to understand when making future decisions

Q: Why is this important?
A: This is important because those memories can guide you if you place them in the right context. If not, they can overrule your emotions. Be careful to not over-react; take your distance, reflect and analyse why they are so important. They might reveal an inner mood that forms part of your identity, or an emotional impact during your youth that later has evolved into a part of yourself, hidden behind many more emotions packed in your archive, but less important. These memories are to be discovered maybe when you start to walk without any purpose and discover the different files in your brain; suddenly you stop and you awake within a non-defined time to realise you were dreaming and have found a very precious moment of your life to use in your future decision-making.

Q: Why?

A: It is good to look to the future. If you use old memories to realise a new dream or project you risk not seeing the contemporary situation. Every day is a new challenge and therefore nostalgia does not help you to see the needs of the future.

5. Store the most valuable everyday emotions

Q: Why?

A: A day is made of moments... hundreds, thousands... if your brain is trained it will archive only those that will serve you later. Don't select, your brain will do this for you. Some everyday memories are important, others are not and they will of course be archives following your emotional state of mind depending on your mood and energy level. The result will be immediate because those archives are working with a very efficient methodology.

6. Write down the memories that are important for the person you are today

Q: How can writing help me?

A: Writing helps your archive to exist. It feels you care about your archive and it will be thankful. Forgetting is human and therefore it can use a bit of support.

7. Use the memories of others but take care not to appropriate them

Q: Why?

A: An archive is not perfect and it might forget to store an important memory. You can ask other archives for information. Don't feel guilty. Be careful not to use them as handed over. Translate them to your own personal experience.

8. Memories are layered; use the layers

Q: How do we use the layers?
A: The memories are all lying one on top of the other. They slowly, slowly form a cube composed of heavier and lighter layers lying upon each other. In this case a heavy layer can oppress the lighter ones. It's up to you to control this situation. My advice is not to ignore your archive but once in a while shake it up and walk through it. It will appreciate this promenade and reorganise a few things automatically.

9. Archives are precious; don't repeat them too often to friends and relatives, they will soon get bored!

Q: How can we avoid this?
A: It happens that you tell a story or recount a special memory because you want to show off. You are tempted to show your friends how rich your archive is. It is common that you use the same files. This is a pity because they will feel your archive is not so rich as you intended. It's good to ask friends... I did talk about this before, didn't I?

10. Your archive is precious! Use it well

Alzheimer's cancels your archive. It deletes your files. So while you are lucky to have it in good health — use it, but use it properly.

She walked into my shop one day and it was like a new wind passing through; a new perfume, a fragrance, an exotic essence. Her name was Christine. She was dressed in white linen and a coloured scarf embroidered with flowers. Her lips painted red and her hair voluminous, flying like her whole appearance. She had just arrived from Hong Kong or India, can't recall, but what I do recall is that she changed my life. She was driving a BMW and came from her office in Ghent where she was working for a cotton company called UCO. She came to buy from my shop, or maybe only for a chat which somehow never stopped. Her lovers needed some trousers and sweaters and she invented some new silhouettes for herself with the enormous wardrobe she had collected over the years. When we travelled to Paris or Japan later she put all her garments into her luggage on hangers and in the hotel room simply opened the suitcases and in five minutes all her clothes were hanging neatly in the cupboard! We had so much fun! Later Christine was working with Dries Van Noten and the business began seriously expanding with shows in Paris. One day when we met I saw she was tired; I had sold my shop in Huidevettersstraat and was only teaching in the Academy of Fashion Design, so I said 'Well, Christine.. if you need me, in Paris or for the sales… I have more time now', and that was the beginning of a very intense period in my life! One of my first trips with her was to Japan, Hong Kong and Taiwan. I saw her blossoming and in her element, talking to old friends, showing me where she once lived in Kowloon. The Peninsula Hotel gave me a shot of luxury and I can still feel the bed, the cushions and the blankets we slept in! Our last day in Hong Kong we had to run through pouring rain and we were both soaked, as if we had taken a shower, that we had to change even our underwear before checking in and taking the next flight. She was bright in all the senses of the word, she was exuberant in every possible and imaginable sense of the word, she was strong and a driving force for many of us. She inspired us with her exoticism and enthusiasm, her intellect and knowledge of how to run a business. When she was getting ill and breast cancer started destroying her, she came to my shop on a Saturday morning and it was like her first confession of the illness. We went to the sea to our small summerhouse and sat on the beach in the sun before she had her first chemotherapy. How can we forget the moments when we knew she found the treatment difficult, and how we supported her to be brave? When she felt better she worked with the same energy and passion again and life went on as before. We had so much fun in Milan where, thanks to the showroom it was as if we were at home and we started to be very comfortable with all the clients and the collections winter / summer… summer / winter… I remember it was my birthday and although we had had an intense day a new client from New York turned up just at the last minute before closing. So she said, do you mind showing him the collection? Yes, of course! No problem, with pleasure. So there I was explaining every detail of the style, fabrics, composition and pointing out some details, but it felt a bit strange to be alone with him. And then his mood changed, he took off his tie, then his shirt and his trousers! No! But then all the team arrived, encouraging him to continue his striptease! We had so much fun! Christine! You were so witty! How much I miss you, your spirit, your joy! We worked hard as well and when I started working with her my first job was to call the clients one by one to come to the showroom in Antwerp, Milan, Paris. We had one phone in our office and the client's data was still on paper files in a wooden box. But how quickly all that was replaced by computers, how quickly the telex machine was replaced by fax and how soon clients became loyal friends buying the powerful collections of Dries! Now I remember some of the garments she wore and they bring memories of moments of joy or pain. I can see her walking to the show dressed with a scarf over a blouse in crème colour silk and a cotton jacket in a beautiful wine-red colour. This exotic flair never left her even when she was wearing black. Christine! We have to live with the presence of the dead, but sometimes we feel the injustice, and then anger takes over and we cannot sleep at night. Talking about Christine is like talking about one of the protagonists of Lawrence Durrell's romance *The Alexandria Quartet*, Justine, Balthazar, Mountolive and Clea, Christine…

Abayah / Achkan / Aesthetic / Agal / Akanjo / Alba / A-Line / Andro Chic / Androgyny / Anorak / Apron / Archetype / Archive / Art Director / Artisan / Asymmetry / Auxetic Fabrics / Avant-garde / Baby Doll / Balaclava / Ball Gown / Baracoa / Bathing Suit / Batik / Beard / Beauty Patch / Bermuda / Bias-Cut / Bikini / Bio Couture / Biodynamic / Biomimetic / Bio-Protection / Blazer / Blogger / Bloomer / Blue-Jeans / Body / Body Stocking / Bolero / Bomber Jacket / Bonnet / Boots / Botox / Boutique / Bow Tie / Bowler / Boxer Shorts / Bracelet / Braguette / Brand identity / Breeches / Bridges / Brocade / Brogue / Buckles / Burnous / Burqa / Bustle / Button Down / Button Hole / Caftan / Calicò / Calotte / Camel Hair / Camouflage / Cape / Capuchon / Cardigan / Cashmere / Casting / Casual / Catwalk / Chador / Chadri / Chaperon Chausses / Chemise / Cheongsam / Chiffon / Chiton / Chlamys / Choker / Chuba / Churidar / Cigarette Shoulders / Circle / Clavi / Cloak / Coat / Cocktail Dress / Codification / Codpiece / Coiffure / Collage / Collar / Colour / Compression Fabrics / Compulsory / Concept Store / Consumerism / Cord-Edging / Corporate Identity / Corsage / Corset / Cosmetics / Cote-hardie / Cotelette / Cotellae / Cotton / Craftsmanship / Cravat / Creative Management / Creativity / Crepe / Crinoline / Cuffs / Culottes / Curating / Dacian Cloak / Dalmatica / Dandy / Darts / Del / Denim / Department Store / Designer / Dhoti / Diadem / Diamonds / Dickey / Digital Dressing / Dirndl / Dishdasha / Display / Disruption / Distortion / Double Breast / Doublet / Draw String / Dress / Duffel Coat / Dummy / Dysfunctional / Earrings / E-Commerce / Edgy / Electroencephalography / Epaulettes / Equity / Erotic / Ethnicity / Evening Wear / Eyeglasses / Eye-Liner / Falbala / Farthingale / Fashion Curating / Fashion Victim / Fast Fashion / Felt / Femininity / Femme Fatale / Fetish / Figure Hugging / Fit

Fitting / Flagship Store / Flax / Flügel / Fourth Sex / Fragrance / Praise / Frock Coat / Fur / Futah / Gandurra / Garde-Corps / Gender / Generation Geometry / Ghaghara / Ghutrah / Gigot Sleeve / Gilet / Girdle / Glocken / Glove / Go / Godet / Gold / Gown / Guerrilla Marketing / Gugel / Gussets Haik / Hair Style / Handbag / Handkerchief / Haori / Harris Tweed / Hat / Haute Couture / Headdress / Hedonistic / Hem / Hénin / Heuke / Hip-Pads Hood / Hooks / Hoops / Horns / Houppelande / Human / Hybrid / Hybrid Holism Couture / Identity / Ikat / Incubator / Indigo / Intelligent Clothing Interlay / Interzone / Intimate / Inuit / Jabot / Jacket / Jacket / Jalkal / Jewelry / Jockstrap / Jodhpur / Journalist / Jumper / Jumpsuit / Junihi-oe / Justaucorps / Kadda / Kalasiris / Kandys / Kansu / Karos / Kasuri Kaunakés / Khatri / Kilt / Kimono / Kirdan / Knickers / Knit / Knitwear / Kosode / Koteka / Kufi / Kurta / Kutiyah / Lace / Laced / Lamba / L'amusse Lapel / Leather / Leggings / Lenderer / Les Incroyables / Linen / Lipstick Live Streaming / Logo / Loincloth / Look Book / Luxury / Luxury Hackers Magazine / Mahoitres / Make Up / Mannequin / Mantle / Maxi Coat / Memory / Merchandising / Microtaggant / Minimal / Mini-Skirt / Mi-Parti / Mitts / Monad / Mono-brand / Monocle / Morphing / Moustache / Mouton Retourné / Multisensory / Muse / Nano-coating / Nanotechnology / Neck-ace / Neoprene / New Look / Nomad / Non Linear / Obi / Old Fashioned / Olfactory / Open Source / Opinion Leader / Outfit / Outlet / Overall / Over-sized / Padding / Paenula / Pannier / Panty-Hose / Pao / Parasol / Parka / Pashmina / Peacock / Peplos / Petticoat / Pied De Poule / Piercing / Plaid Plastic Surgery / Pluviale / Pointed Shoes / Polka Dot / Polo / Polonaise / Pompon / Poncho / Pop-Up / Poulaine / Pourpoint / Prêt-A-Porter / Prince Of Wales Check / Prototype / Puff-Sleeve Jacket / Pullover / Punk / Push-

p / Pyjamas / Quixie / Qumbaz / Raincoat / Reactive Surfaces / Recycle
Red Carpet / Redingote / Renaissance / Reversible / Ribbon / Riding
Boots / Ring / Robe / Sack Sleeves / Saharienne / Salon / Salwar Kameez
Samurai / Sandal / Sans-culottes / Sari / Sarong / Schecke / Schecken-
rock / Schenti / Sculpt Sizing / Sculpted Skin / Season / Second Hand
Second Skin / Seem / Semicircular / Sensory Textiles / Sensuality / Sewing
Machine / Sexy / Shaman / Shaping / Sharp-Memory / Shawl / Shearling
Shibori / Shoe Tree / Shopping / Sinus / Sjamberloek / Sketch / Skirt / Skul
Slashing / Sleeve Holes / Sleeves / Slip / Slippers / Slow Fashion / Smar
Garment / Smell / Smock / Snap-Fasteners / Sneakers / Socks / Soutane
Spacesuit / Spaghetti Straps / Stiletto / Stockings / Stola / Stomache
Street Style / Style / Style Icon / Suckenie / Sunglasses / Surçot / Sus
penders / Sustainable / Sweat-proof / Tabard / Tabi / Tagelmust / Tail-Coa
Tailor / Talaris Dalmatica / Tappert / Tarbush / Tartan / Tattoo / Technol-
ogy / Temporariness / Termochromic / Textile Industry / Thimble / Thobe
Three D-Printing / Throw-Away Chic / Tiara / Tie / Tie-Dye / Tikka / Toga
Top-Hat / Toque / Total Look / Trademark / Transe-For-M-tion / Trend
Trend Forecasting / Trend-Hungry / Trendy / Tribe / Trimmings / Trousers
Tundra Jacket / Tunica Angusticlavia / Tunica Intima / Tunica Laticlavia
Tunica Palmata / Turtleneck / Tuxedo / Twin-Set / Ubala Abuyisse / Uhm
wpe Fibres / Umbrella / Unconstructed / Under-Garment / Under-Shoe
Unfinished / Uniform / Unisex / Up-To-Date / Urban Camouflage / Urbar
Security Suit / Urbanism / Veil / Velvet / Vertugadin / Vest / Virtual Design
Visionaries / Visionary / Vitaminised Textiles / V-Shaped Neck / Waistcoat
Waistline / Wammes / Water-Soluble PVA / Watteau / Weaver / Weightless
Wig / Wool / Yuzen / Zeitgeist / Zhongshan / Zip / Zori

Dirk

THERE IS ANOTHER WAY OF LOOKING AT THINGS
LANGUAGE ALLOWS US TO CREATE NEW THOUGH
TS TO INTERACT WITH OTHERS TO CHANGE IN EV
ERY MOMENT OF OUR LIVES EVERYWHERE IN THE
REAL WORLD THE HUMAN LONGING FOR FREEDOM
REQUIRES AN UNDERSTANDING OF DIFFERENT LA
NGUAGES AND CULTURES DIFFERENT ATTITUDES
DIFFERENT TIMES AND PLACES ALL OF WHICH SPE
AK OF THE SAME HUMAN NEEDS AND ASPIRATIONS
THERE IS ANOTHER WAY OF LOOKING AT THINGS

Maurizio Nannucci
There is another way of looking -
Musée d'Art moderne et contemporain
de Saint-Étienne Métropole 2012

or years I was in a state of unconsciousness graced by the instinct of knowing what to do and not to do. Not only did I never look for a job, but the job came to me instead. So I tumbled from being a designer to a retailer, from a retailer to a teacher, from a teacher to a builder of bridges, from a window dresser to an events' organiser to a distributor, a stylist, a museum director, a director, a visionary, a curator… a dreamer but mostly a doer. Propose a challenging job to me and I will go for it. I find the path and the direction that create growth, I will design a strategy, make a business plan and budget for making miracles happen, transforming an institute, a museum, a school or even a house or a shop into a flamboyant and attractive, eye-catching project. My book is a book for understanding my own creativity and eventually to inspire others to use their own without fear. Transcribing my experiences has helped me to understand my personal path because through art, architecture and space and thanks to the people have met and spoken to, indeed, especially to those encounters, I might be surprised to discover that my instinct and my intuition were and are my guide. Maybe this reflexion can help me understand what went wrong or what should be done in fashion, art and architecture to rediscover the emotional impact that it can have on the world. The most intriguing and the mos interesting chapter of my life is the one I live to-day in Florence. First, because now that I have discovered the freedom of writing, I quite like the risk of making mistakes; second, because by writing I am discovering my own thoughts and doubts and this is quite challenging. Maybe there will be some delusion if I find that what I did was not so captivating or interesting at all! No problem. Everything I have done was honest and fearless because I believe in a categorical and rigorous approach in life. I believe in night and day dreams… That's why I am writing this book.

From 1965 to 1971 I was studying Fashion Design at the Royal Academy of Fine Arts. I was a good student… not remarkable, but good. I struggled with making garments, although my father and grandfather were tailors, and I was probably not so focused. But I did an internship at Bartsons raincoat manufacturer before graduating. So, you see, Madame Prijot, my teacher, recognised in me the fast and dynamic person I later became. The inspiration for my final-year collection of twelve outfits was African masks.

I watched *2001: A Space Odyssey*, the film by director Stanley Kubrick, with my future husband in 1968. I watched the landing of Armstrong on the moon in July 1969. I was married by that time. Both events were moments. In Italian *Casa Vogue* I stared at a house designed by Tadao Ando. Living in concrete and in a minnal environment, the way the light was falling in the house, the simple sitting room, the one tree that disturbed the harmony was an important moment in my aesthetic perception. I discovered more of Tadao Ando's minimalist approach and the use of space, light and nature in the Koshino House. That might be the reason why in 1969 when we married, my husband and I chose the white furniture of Joe Colombo the table and the chairs and the wooden chairs I later gave to my friend Raf Simons. This futuristic approach — living in a white environment — gave us, I guess, an open mind-set.

My portable transistor Braun T26 radio with leather strap changed my life! I was listening to those French songs! I understood half of it but it didn't matter. I understood all of it. I was wearing black high-neck sweaters; I was romantic and dreamy and listened to the songs of Juliette Greco, Barbara (*L'Aigle noir*), Charles Aznavour, Yves Montand (*Les Feuilles mortes*) Georges Brassens. The one who touched me the most was Léo Ferré ('Avec le temps, va tout s'en va…'). His French language was enigmatic, nostalgic, strong and intriguingly beautiful. As I am writing and researching now, I have discovered the album where he plays the piano and recites the poems of Baudelaire — *Les Fleurs du mal (suite et fin)*.

When I look back at this period in my youth I feel it was probably the most significant because it shaped my personality; dark, lonely brutal, always in search for something, maybe for quality-based solutions, maybe because of a critical attitude or maybe because not really a team player or a nice little girl. In a way, sport was a saviour, especially tennis and golf. Tennis, because my parents founded the tennis club and it was an escape from the city to the countryside: first Kapellen, later Brasschaat. Tennis is a lonely sport. You are alone in front of your competitor. Two solutions: either you win or you lose; golf, because there are only two solutions; either you play well or you play badly; for me it was mostly the second choice, because golf is a lot of practise and concentration. It is though a nice walk in a beautiful landscape, and playing with friends or with my husband was sometimes relaxing. Social life in clubs is tricky and therefore not suited for me.

It's true, I never liked to play in team such as, hiding in gardens at birthday parties with children, or playing carts, or playing darts or Monopoly or having fun making cakes. I was always crying when my parents said yes to the invitation ad the dramas arrived when the hour came to go to the party. Where does this loneliness comes from? I didn't received comic strips from my parents and therefore I am not receptive for fun and laughter. I married a guy that has good humour though; he makes me laugh! Oefa!!! he saved me from a boring life! My parents wanted me to go to university, the chance they never had because of the Second World War. I had to study Latin and Greek, mathe-

...matics and science and geography in a primary school at Mechelsesteenweg. In the classroom I listened to teachers and was expected to remember and repeat what they were saying. I was not really interested in those lessons and had difficulty studying in my room at home. I was always drawing. My mother, who understood my attraction to art, took the wise decision to enrol me at the art school for a three-year preparation course in Artistic Humanities. At the age of 15 I was the best student in the class, the prettiest, the most creative, the most dynamic... the happiest. I could express myself making installations for the annual festivities at Carnival time and worked on many more projects. I listened, fascinated, to Hubert Dethier, my teacher of ethics and aesthetics in the arts, humanism and freethinking, and to excellent teachers of art history... I learned perspective drawing the nude, and became the person I am now. My friends studied the monumental arts, painting, and architecture and I was hoping to enter the interior design or architecture department after my humanities course. Destiny decided my life would take another direction, fashion!

This loneliness has great advantages. It gives you time and space to reflect on your job and on your social engagement and fashion is useful for understanding society. It creates tension and tension is needed for achieving success thanks to ambition. Don't enter the inferno if you are not motivated to succeed. Lonely people compose the fashion family. Every single member has a strong ego and even when working to achieve the success of the designer you work within the rules and they are played hard. Competition is in the air and there are hardly new shops opening. Economics are key for success and if you are afraid of numbers be careful, don't step in in the world of fashion!

Timeline

The Cities that Made Me

'On the table beside me as I write lies my steamship ticket to France; yesterday I knew with absolute certainty that I must go there. Do you remember Pursewarden used to say that artists, like sick cats, knew by instinct exactly which herb they needed to affect the cure and that the bitter-sweet herb of their self-discovery only grew in one place, France? Within 10 days I will be gone! And among so many new certainties there is one which has raised its head — the certainty that you will follow me there in your good time.'

Lawrence Durrell, The Alexandria Quartet, *fourth book, Clea, p. 279*

It's time for change; Florence, Antwerp... they gave me and Dirk a lot; friendship, sunsets, work, dreams, success, houses and passions. But it is time for change. Like cats we are going to look for new herbs; not that we feel sick, but maybe we are a bit tired. We need large avenues, large views, large markets and large museums or large cafés and terraces. Maybe we need new chairs and tablecloths, new handkerchiefs and new spoons and knives, new cushions and new books. We need new walks and new hairdressers, new trains who will bring us to new cities. We need new recipes and new suns and new rain.

Change is good. We enjoyed Florence tremendously. I personally looked at art and renaissance in a different perspective and discovered why and when architects, urbanists, engineers were working in Florence and why Galileo Galilei walking thru our garden looked at the sky and discovered so much about our solar system. We absorbed it all with eagerness and a hunger for understanding the city's history and eventual future gave us new ideas for food, travel, work and quality of life.

The question remains though: what is the future project designed for a city such as Florence? The beautiful landscape is also a beautiful limitation for growth. Tourists take over, a hundred thousand a day like insects, eating and drinking, making selfies before the Duomo. Brunelleschi prepared himself many years for he knew he himself was the only person able to design the dome for the unfinished cathedral. Believe is vision, vision, study, knowledge are crowned thanks to believe. But what remains of this enormous realisation? Mostly guided tours and thousand of pictures on Facebook and Instagram and a narrative for a cheap and superficial film. Cynical is that the main theme of Dan Brown's *Inferno* is about overpopulation while filming in an overpopulated city, Florence. Well, maybe this is an over-critical comment.

We have to follow our instinct for giving knowledge away. That's why I gave so much to Antwerp, the city I loved so dearly! I was so proud to show my city to all the people we were working with when starting this new fashion movement. I myself turned into a guide, showing the cathedral, the Rubens paintings in the museum, the port which I loved tremendously because of the greatness of the setting, the lightning at night, the docks and the boats, the cargos and the cranes! Invited to Antwerp by Dries to buy the collection, people from all over the world arrived, sometimes also as judges in the annual shows of the Academy, or passing by as journalists writing on new cities to be discovered because city trips were in. They loved the food, the rain even and the shopping. Saying this about Antwerp I can repeat the same enthusiasm for Florence, although a shorter but maybe even more intensive period gave me the enthusiasm for absorbing the light, the sunset, the bridges, the palazzo and the parties in those same palazzos. Dan Brown's thriller recreated recently the inferno Dante Alighieri described so well in the first chapter of his Divina Commedia. Some taxi drivers are repeating the words and rhymes of Dante while driving!

will remember Florence using the three metaphors of Dante Alighieri: Hell, Purgatory and Paradise. I will put them in a different order starting with Paradise. Paradise meant to me a dream-like state of mind during the first three years in Florence; our life was dominated by the beauty of the landscape, learning new methods for living in a warm countryside. Friends visiting us and staying amazed on our balcony looking at the garden and at night to the night flies or the moon so bright you hardly could believe it. We made new friendships and Dirk started editing films again! But above all he started cooking! And how! Unbelievable inventive, the most complex dishes with passion and determination!

Purgatory stands for the three following years where I discovered the freedom for managing a team, and reorganising didactics. We developed a strong vision and thanks to the vision we attracted interesting people to study at Polimoda or teach and discuss the future of education, the future of the city and not only. Those were the happy days. The *Momenting the Memento* book was born and written in 2012 by Danilo Venturi, a concept to be realised later in a one-week conference in 2015. Those were the most creative days of personal and common achievement and success. The last three years became an inferno, working hard, with concentration, determination but rather difficult for different reasons and changes to be done at least; for living in a city interested in tourism and festivals instead in the support of a new cultural movement became hard to accept. But let me clarify Hell; it was a nice hell, full of challenges and eventual great steps forwards to achieve a new Paradise. This is what hell should be and why it has been created. It might have been a bit more crowded in hell; it was a bit lonely; we were too few to make it turn in a big party Working of the IFFII confer-

Once we created hell on earth, we had a hard time because we knew our project was too ambitious. Sleepless nights, different visions, different methods, different techniques; five people working like hell, but we made it. When the project finished and the five days were over there was only a little joy; what remained was a depression. The trauma of having achieved something special and not really being able to capture the real success, this created a void. It seems normal after a so strong concentration of workload, images, feelings, words, hugs and maybe criticism. Some courage is needed to go on, to make a catalogue even better than the event itself. We did it.

Dirk looking at our past

Jannis Kounellis, 1973 - Venice Biennale 1978
Untitled - still from video

OPINION

Dress / Body / Calligraphy / Craft / Space / Imagery

Why do I avoid speaking about fashion? The word 'fashion' was banned in the conference. It didn't cover the initial meaning; beauty, elegance, pattern design and refined aesthetics. Fashion became vulgar and fashion magazines without content. Here I guess I have to explain. I used six words avoiding the word fashion. I asked myself a few questions, like: what can we do to enjoy creativity; how can we embrace, inspire, encourage creativity; how can we discover creativity; how do we select creative minds; how and why are we searching for creativity?

Here below my opinion piece...

DRESS Especially during art fairs, art biennales, fashion weeks or festivals of different disciplines our sixth sense is more attentive. We are in search of a new hype, a new style or a different aesthetic, a new emotion, or what I call 'moments'. And so, in the fashion world, when we are happy with a more sensual and feminine Gucci for men, a more deconstructed silhouette for Raf Simons, and a sleeker silhouette for Givenchy menswear that pleases women as well, we have a positive reaction to the world we live in. And if Walter Van Beirendonck says 'stop terrorising our world' we agree, because we have just experienced a wake-up call about freedom of expression and a religious perception of what freedom might mean to each of us. And when we see a new expression of our body language, or dress to be reborn in a more abstract concept, then we feel history might be ready for a new experience or a new decade of creativity. The 21st century has not brought great innovations and therefore we are just copying and pasting the old ones. We are not creating new ones and that might signal the start of decadence in our society. And if we look at past generations and past decades we still like our ancestors, their stories, their dreams, their disappointments, their drugs and decadence, and their naivety. We must overcome the dangerous memories and stop living amidst nostalgia for the past.

BODY We are looking for the next art or architecture biennale and we dream and discuss the titles and the curators. They will give us the answers! Pavilions will again be our meeting points to create the moments in which we recognise our personal cultural attachments, linked to the place where we were born. Manifestos will be launched and talks organised, discussions and open platforms will be programmed to initiate the debate about art — is it still relevant? Does it reflect society? — bringing wise and experienced visionaries together. During these encounters we try to understand the future, often because we look to the past. Here our body and our body language are the only ways to express our fears and dreams; they can suggest solutions for the suffering, the questions, the uncertainties of the world we live in surrounded by war and terror. We use our body to express those fears and to connect with an audience that is also searching... searching... should we all follow the master classes of Carolyn Carlson to understand better the functions and possible uses of our body?

CALLIGRAPHY We live the hybridisation of a liquid society. A hybrid society is one that comprises a range of social and cultural influences and components, rather than having a homogenous identity. A liquid society is defined by its fragility, its temporariness, its vulnerability and inclination to constant flow and change. Thanks to the liquid society we are hybrid, we are multiverse; we are a set of infinite or finite possible universes comprising everything that exists such as space, time, matter, and energy... we are visible but simultaneously invisible; we are versatile, but also liquid. We are multi but also one. We write more but do we write better? This might be a nonsense question but the speed of the life we live is responsible for our superficiality and fragility; remember we are liquid and search for constant change. Marcel Broodthaers chose art as an expression because of his failure as a writer; the juxtaposition of text and image becomes poetry. The question of the meaning of art, querying the venue of the exhibition, the role of the gallery, querying too the institution of the museum and its functions are all part of art itself. Broodthaers says, 'For me, film is an extension of language. I began with poetry, then visual art, and finally cinema, which brings together several different elements of art. Writing (poetry), the object (visual art) and the image (video or film) are brought together'. The example of Broodthaers is important for understanding the different meanings of the act of writing. In China calligraphy is an art itself and has to be improved by repetition to refine the skill that gives the word its expression. Cobra used writing as painting and painting often means writing a colour or expressing a mood or communicating a manifesto. The artist On Kawara expresses moments by painting a date on a canvas. Dante became a pha[r]macist because, at the time of the Middle Ages, books were sold from apothecary shops. Writing about art, design, fashion, dance, literature has become merely reporting what one sees and not what one feels. We write about the style, colour, line, shape, volume, size and texture, but do we write about the essence of the work? Can we start a debate about what calligraphy can teach us to be a better writer?

SPACE We are surrounded by architecture. Some buildings were made 3000 years ago, others date from the last decade, built by Zaha Hadid or Frank Gehry. We are living in those earlier monuments, cloisters, palaces or previous temples. Ou Ning, Chinese activist, art director, writer, is escaping from big cities such as Beijing or Shanghai and is going back to the rural environment of Bishan. He is a part of the Rural Reconstruction Movement. Can we choose the act of construction and reconstruction? Are we able to build spaces we can inhabit, use as institutes for education or for museum activities without disturbing skylines? What do we conserve and what is to be destroyed? Is history the right driver for conservation? Is the Santa Croce basilica a history book for art and architecture lovers or is it a tool for reading history in a contemporary context? From the simplicity of Giotto to the dramatic tombs of the Romantics we are surrounded by clashes of history and we are confused. Does this collage reflect the actual state in which the cities of the world are growing and creating an ever more complex urbanistic chaos? Some houses in far away cultures are still today built by hand with ice, leaves, wood or plaster, but handicrafts are disappearing. Hands are becoming useless. We use three-D, scanning and super technologies to show us our way around unknown cities. Drones follow every step we make and we feel that is ok. We are not anonymous, we are multiple, and we are both universe and universal.

CRAFT Last but not least we reflect on craft, the noble art of creating an object, a form, a material, a liquid, or simply a pot or a vase. We are seeking to preserve this art as we find it is disappearing as a result of its insignificance to our modern word. The speed of our society leaves no time or place for craft. The slow pace and processes are not acceptable to our new way of thinking, working, dreaming. Craftsmen are lone individuals, slowly facing isolation. We are global and global seems to be linked to loneliness. Industrialisation changed our perception of time and centuries later we are again fascinated by the undiscovered potential of science and scientific research. We are fascinated by the capacities of our new devices, our new communication tools, and our supernatural technologies by which we are connected. The sky is the limit. Researchers are giving us endless surprises but these are only the beginning of what our imagination can do. We are torn between the lack of slowness and the longing for fastness. We are addicted to this new technology that offers us a new human and trans human relationship. The artist is the thinker and he uses craftsmen to realise their dream.

IMAGERY

THE (HYBRID)ISATION OF THE LIQUID SOCIETY
A hybrid society is a society that comprises a range of social and cultural influences and components, rather than having a homogenous identity.

A liquid society is defined by its fragility, its temporariness, its vulnerability and inclination to constant change.

Thanks to the liquid society we are hybrid, WE ARE MULTIVERSE.

WE ARE MULTIVERSE, because we are a set of infinite or finite possible universes that together comprise everything that exists such as space, time, matter, and energy…

We are visible < we are invisible
We are versatile < we are liquid
We are multi < we are one

I. WWW

THANKS TO THE WWW WE KNOW MORE
THANKS TO THE WWW WE ARE CONNECTED
THANKS TO THE WWW WE LIVE IN DIFFERENT WORLDS
THANKS TO THE (HYBRID)ISATION WE ARE MULTIVERSE
THANKS TO THE WWW WE ARE MULTI CULTURAL
WE ARE THE '89PLUS LAYERED GENERATION SOCIETY

II. QUESTIONS

We travel more, but do we travel better?
We eat more, but do we eat better?
We learn more, but do we learn better?
We discuss more, but do we discuss better?
We live more, but do we live better?
We buy more, but do we buy better?
We are social, but are we?

WE ARE A COLLAGE

The writing becomes a drawing, and the word becomes an image...

Shops & Schools are learning laboratories...

Stereotypes are gone... we think more freely. Fashion becomes the cultural platform we were looking for...

The next city is Bishan (like a new back-to-the-land lifestyle) by Ou Ning... Ou Ning; the New Rural Reconstruction Movement; we mainly work on historical preservation, cultural production and public life in the village...

The next fashion designer is Ma Ke...

'Art & Fashion' can save the world. 'Art, Fashion and **Education**' can save the world...

We can analyse the past to predict the future. We are forecasters... Intelligence is created by people, groups, tribes and cultures...

We must dream; the future is composed by dreams...

IV. CONCLUSION

Danilo Venturi wrote: 'The Internet, the downfall of ideologies and globalisation made geography (space) become irrelevant, therefore history too (time). In every decade of the last century fashion produced a main style that the industry keeps on re-editing in terms of heritage or vintage. Well, the first decade of the new millennium didn't produce any style and in the future we won't have anything to re-produce. It's a crisis of values that generates also an economic one. This is scary but also a great opportunity. It means the time has come for authorship again, for producing new moments (*Momenting*) to be remembered (*Memento*). The problem is how. My idea is to look at the pasts that never became futures and to produce futures that don't have any past for justification'.

DANILO VENTURI, *MOMENTING THE MEMENTO*

A 'MOMENT' WHERE WE ARE INSPIRED TO THINK, WRITE, AND DESIGN THE FUTURE

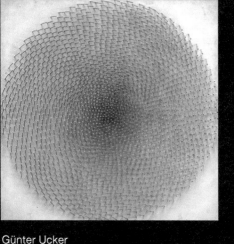

Günter Ucker
Spiral, 1997
Museum voor Schone Kunsten Antwerp
© Lukas - Art in Flanders, photo Hugo Martens

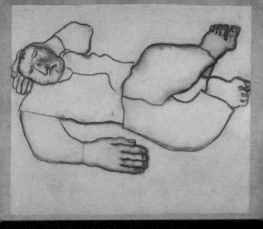

Constant Permeke
Sleeping Peasant, 1928
Museum voor Schone Kunsten Gent
© Lukas - Art in Flanders, photo Hugo Martens

I am not sure if May '68 had a certain effect on my eventual approach to life or if it was my Italian grandfather who caused me to feel detached from any specific society. Let's first consider May '68 — that phenomenon of students rebelling against education which was stuck in rigid conservatism. Awards such as the Prix de Rome in Paris were abolished, the Cannes Festival did not take place, some pavilions of the Venice Biennale closed their doors and no award was given, while museums in Paris shut for fear of vandalism. The Nouvelle Vague in French cinema had already been active for many years, and Truffaut and Godard were the protagonists of this new language and rebellious attitude. Young and inexperienced filmmakers, they had the nerve to invite Hitchcock and other film directors to Paris because they had watched their films in secret admiration. The icon system worked! Students boycotted lessons and developed manifestos in protest. The anti-political movement was more aggressive, shouting at de Gaulle, fearing repressive behaviour, their vision and fight was for a more left and democratic society. Architects, filmmakers, museum directors, teachers, artists, actors, musicians, writers supported the movement. Posters such as 'Les Beaux-Arts sont fermés mais l'Art Revolutionnaire est né' were posted in the streets. I was also in the streets in '68 and am still proud of that moment although I was not so angry. The Academy of Fine Arts in Antwerp had introduced Applied Arts where I was surrounded by interesting teachers and felt a certain liberation after a more conventional Latin and Greek high school education. I think the Nouvelle Vague and the existentialist movement when I was younger also pushed me into the arms of the filmmaker Dirk, bearded and walking on the lawn with a pipe in his mouth; I was more attracted to his humour and cynical speech than to the more conventional boys at the University. Then probably that innate Italian spirit made me different. My black hair, my dark and angry side, my solitude, my critical eye sometimes made me a loner. Not in the

Academy where I felt at home. We married in 1969. This was our act of liberation. Our little flat, our modern furniture, my white Courrèges-like dress, our wedding at the town hall, taking a number in a queue like in a shop nowadays made it all low-key but fun. It came as a shock when we realised that my husband had to do military service. Luckily his ears were a problem and this saved the situation as he was not accepted. He being a film director life was exciting and sometimes unpredictable, but that actually suited the way we thought life should be. I thank my parents and my husband's parents for their understanding and for supporting the couple we were.

Timeline

Drawing the nude

Drawing the nude is like drawing a letter or a symbol. You look at lines, shadows, and proportions; you see volumes, absences, gaps or depths. You forget the body and slowly, slowly you are in a very special state of mind. The lines are soft in the beginning but the more you gaze the more you draw highlights; your fingers touch the paper, you have to feel the charcoal, you need to get your hands dirty and work into the subject. There is nothing left except silence, the world outside has gone, the silence is disturbing, and light is your companion. You get tired but are fulfilled. Your back hurts, your arms move and then you step back, take your distance and contemplate the naked body and the body on the paper. Then you get angry and disappointed, desperate for not having the lines right or because you see volumes you didn't see before. The body moves and therefore the person is real, the contact grows, the lines soften and the anger is gone. There is a lot to add but there is even more to cancel. The shadows fill the voids and three dimensions begin to appear... the writing starts, the subtle grows, the more you look, the more you see. Nothing is like before... you relax, you dream away...

Pavilions

Pavilions are buildings without a specific function. Mostly built to host the best innovations of mankind; inventions, explorations, discoveries, sound or imagery, temporary exhibitions for visitors curious to see or show to their children and grandchildren what man is capable of. But pavilions out-live the event and then they start a second life. They serve as event halls or museums or parks for children or companies looking for a smart and off-beat location. World exhibitions are full of pavilions; they cost a lot of money and sometimes I ask myself if this all is worth it. Pavilions represent a nation, a culture, a moment in time. They tell history. If you go to the Art Biennale in Venice, you visit your own pavilion! And you are very proud of it, especially when you feel the artist is good, and the curator too. The first foreign pavilion was that of Belgium built in 1907 under the initiative of Prof. Fierens-Gevaert, the Belgian general director of Fine arts during the reign of King Leopold II. On the renewed façade you can read L'UNION FAIT LA FORCE. Today it looks as a very cynical statement as the country is divided politically and culturally in several pieces of land, language and economical success and the slogan was recently in decay symbolically by nature or activated by the handling of men, who knows? Art Nouveau and geometry were inspirations for Belgian architects; Hoffmann designed and constructed the Palais Stoclet in Brussels, a masterpiece of Art Nouveau style and a proud beacon for Belgians reunited by art and architecture. The pavilions themselves form a sort of anthology of important 20th-century architecture — given they were designed by architects of the status of Aalto, Hoffmann, Rietveld, Scarpa and Stirling.

Visiting the 56th Art Biennale curated by Okwui Enwezor in 2015 I re-dis-covered the purity of the Austrian pavilion designed by Hoffmann in 1934. The building has no main entrance, but it's like entering a void that ends in a garden that reflects the pavilion that reflects again the geometry and symmetry of the poetic spaces thanks to the light or shadows created by nature. The artist intervention of Heimo Zoberling for this Biennale was in complete harmony combining form and content. Visitors didn't always capture this nothingness entering and leaving the pavilion disappointed for not having seen a work of art.

Sensing spaces

The sub-title of my book, *Fragments of Life,* could be altered in *Fragments of Spaces*. My strongest memories are based on the first impact entering a space that brings me to the essentials of life itself. I can sense the space, the spirituality of the place, the scale of humility of the space created by its volumes, the presence of light, the absence of work or the absence of sound.

Such as the pavilions in the Venice Biennale, the exhibition *Sensing Spaces: Architecture Reimagined* at the Royal Academy of Arts, London, in April 2014, wanted to evoke the experience of architecture within a gallery environment of the Royal Academy. The constructions of six architects were the starting point for the visitor to undergo and understand or question their own ideas about architecture and create new sensations to inhabit spaces or private houses beyond the gallery walls. A very ambitious project where six studio architects— Yvonne Farell and Shelley Mc Namara of Grafton Architects, Kengo Kuma from Kanagawa, Japan, Diébédo Francis Kéré from Burkina Faso, Li Xiaodong from China, Sofia von Ellrichshausen and Maurizio Pezo from Chile, and finally Eduardo Souto de Moura Alvaro Siza from Portugal — created volumes full of light and mist. Exhibitions are testing grounds, areas of experimentation (see Philip Ursprung, *Presence: The Light Touch of Architecture*, catalogue of the exhibition *Sensing Spaces*).

The two architects of Crafton Architects define themselves as 'space-makers'. They say: as architects we imagine or structure space. They say architecture should provide enjoyment and comfort. I have felt those values in Japan while visiting a Japanese temple or house, but also when looking at the horizon sitting on the beach. The seascapes and photography of Hioshi Sugimoto capture this sense of absolute contemplation and serenity

The exhibition in London allowed children, adults, architects and lovers of spaces to playfully enjoy what architecture is actually all about. Without great rhetoric or theoretical texts on the wall, people experienced the different rooms. Walking in the labyrinth of wooden walls to emerge in a bigger mirrored room, to contemplate what the Chinese architect Li Xiaodong says — 'Space is perceived through a dialogue between imagination and reality' — the purpose of the exhibition became more and more an interesting experiment. What was defined in the Han Dynasty, about 2000 years ago, has been slowly slowly embedded in our western culture. Li Xiaodong says that the ancient Chinese philosopher Lao Zi states that what is important is what it contained, not the container. His own research is therefore focused on exploring whether contemporary architecture could be enriched through dialogue with his ancient tradition. Personally I feel very attracted to the empty space and the fact content is created within. Our loft, designed and build in the 1980s was a great example of this exercise for a living thanks to the essential volumes composed by concrete and light. Now I am conscious that our personal living spaces became bigger and bigger during the years, but that they will become smaller and smaller the older we become.

Space is perceived through a dialogue between imagination and reality.

Li Xiaodong

The Casa Poli in Chile, the first project of the architects Mauricio Pezo and Sofia Von Ellrichshausen, has this ambiguity — neither a house nor a pavilion but a combination of both. This house is the utmost perfection of what intellectual rationalism and sensitive architecture should be. For *Sensing Spaces* the wooden construction with the staircase to climb had a strong impact witnessing the history and the building of the Academy

Linda at the Venice Biennale,
Belgian Pavilion, 1995

Dirk at the Venice Biennale,
Belgian Pavilion, 1995

Pavilions for Education

For education I dream of The Laboratory; a meeting point, where 'creatives' of many different disciplines can discuss with scientists or with great industrial leaders to define the future of the 'Creative Industries'. It is a space where we will talk, write, discuss, ask questions, find temporary answers that will provoke new questions. Maybe my houses, pavilions, schools, offices, shops, museums were such places, but now it is time to destroy the walls that divided all these spaces and bring them together under one roof. Education cannot be locked in classrooms where students listen and teachers speak from 9a.m. to 7p.m. Education has to keep breaking the rules, exploring knowledge and absorbing what is found. The search for knowledge must be a dialogue. Space is important, an open space, a 'Palais de Tokyo' space, where we play, sing, dance, or simply contemplate images, write, educate, experiment, sew, knit, and create objects, not garments. A place where we make 'The House of the Future'. We start by looking for scaffoldings of wood, stone, metal frames, glass or we simply begin building something like the artist Von Ellrichshausen — to construct the dream location for education. The Serpentine Gallery has a pavilion designed in 2014 by the Chilean architect Smiljan Radic. Poetry, debates, talks are exactly what pavilions are built for. Museums should have pavilions where we can discuss the exhibition we just visited. I feel I need my own pavilion where I can invite friends, philosophers, artists, fashion designers, and sit together having conversations. And there is a lot to debate; I interview a lot of people who visit the laboratory next to my office. I ask general questions but the answers are very focused. In general, people travel a lot and while travelling they define their vision. Experiences are becoming more intense and more faceted every day. Probably we sleep less, and think more. Maybe it will result in a small space of 50 square metres. I need to talk to people, timeless talks maybe not even recorded; simple talks on simple subjects. Maybe pavilions in the Biennale should be as such. They would probably end up in endless discussions about politics of how culture is diploid or used and misused.

My Linda Loppa Pavilion

My Linda Loppa pavilion will be a room where light and sound can flow and change. We could sit on the floor or we could lie down on mattresses or stand upright or sit on benches. We could ask people to write a page on a specific topic and then discuss it for a few hours; we can record the conversations and then make them into a publication because the printed paper is still poetic. Like Francesco de' Medici we will invite artists, politicians and poets to discuss the future of art, its ethics and aesthetics. We can have pavilions in many different cities. We can have them in schools, institutes, gardens, museums, galleries, private homes; they can have different shapes and volumes according to the location. They should bring all generations together because there is no generation gap. We are all internauts... we all travel and speak five or more languages and English is our common language. We will be invited all over the world to put our pavilion in a square or a museum, or gallery, and start the debate because we have to talk more. The Linda Loppa pavilion will be black or white and will be equipped with beamers, audio, a small kitchen and floor heating. There will be neon light but we will use candlelight as well, or cosy lamps. We will need writers who will be able to capture our discussions and turn them into a philosophy. We will write manifestoes because we know that we will have to be convincing for a generation informed by the media! But we will be educated and not naïve; our vision will be based on knowledge, experience and research.

The world Expo '58 in Brussels was about modern architecture! I was 10 years old. There were pavilions! Many! The Russian one made a big impact on me because it had the Sputnik! It had gone to space and come back and you could admire this new metal engine that could fly! The American pavilion was also impressive; it later became a studio for TV shows with the presenter Tony Corsari. I stepped into the cable cars and saw the landscapes and pavilions from above. The Multivision film and sound pavilion was fabulous! Sound travelled from one end to the other — it was a great innovation! The pavilions were all magnificent! And the Atomium! At night the nine spheres of the Atomium statue twinkled in the sky. There were also a lot of African pavilions and because Belgium had colonised the Congo, I could see Africans performing ritual dances!

Pavilions

Antwerp Zoo

The zoo is full of pavilions. The zoo is two minutes away from the Central Station and to me it was a wonderful promenade around exotic landscapes and animals. Entering the zoo the flamingos welcomed you graciously before you would visit Jules, the enormous orang-utan who watched you from behind glass. He could speak with his eyes. He was sometimes angry because he was locked up in the cage, but he made friends with those of us who came to visit him and also with his guardian. He became a real citizen of Antwerp. In the open air were the smaller apes and an enormous hippopotamus. The aquarium was really amazing! It smelled humid and it was warm and fascinating. The replica of an Egyptian temple where the giraffes looked down on you from above, and the elephants you could feed, were absolutely fabulous; those were of course the most amazing experiences. Lions and also white bears lived in the open air in monumental structures near the Central Station and you could hear the sound of the trains departing and arriving. Later, when I was studying art in the humanities foundation courses before entering the Art Academy itself, I often went there to draw; I had a little chair, a wooden box with my pencils and watercolour paints and sat down drawing. Oh, I forgot, there were the aviaries where multi-coloured exotic birds would shout at you.

Pavilions

Parks

Central park in Antwerp, near the Diamond Centre, is a beautiful nostalgic park with a lake, a bridge, and fine sculptures. I walked there as a child, and later as an inhabitant of the centre of Antwerp. The Jardin de Tuileries in Paris has the same relaxing effect on people. The same happened to me in Hyde Park and at the Serpentine Gallery. To experience the beauty of nature in a city is very precious. The gardens of Tokyo and Kyoto have the same effect on me. I enjoy nature in contrast with the city more than living in the green countryside.

Pavilions

Open-Air Museums

The Middelheim open-air museum is in a park and it has a beautiful pavilion built by the Belgian architect Renaat Braem in 1971. This too is a nonsense space conceived for hosting temporary exhibitions. A fascinating building in a park.

Pavilions

San Francesco di Paola

From our terrace we see a pavilion on the road that leads to our neighbours. Now people come in their cars, on motorcycle or bicycle but as the road is quite high very few people come by foot. None of them uses the pavilion that was probably built around 1900 to provide a rest before continuing up the hill. Who knows what kind of romances began in the pavilion? Have we forgotten to sit for a while and contemplate the landscape? Many gardens have pavilions and we don't use them anymore. They are neglected mementoes of a past that was more romantic. We are shut up in our rooms, behind a desk searching on blogs for news. Instead, we could sit in a pavilion to discuss the topic of a particular lesson on fashion management. The result of that discussion would probably have a greater impact on the student's future vision; the teacher would have better contact with the individual sitting with him or her in the pavilion. We are talking about Nietzsche and Proust, about Karl Marx and *Das Kapital*, because Okwui Enzewor, the curator of the 2015 Art Biennale in Venice, asked us to do so. Philosophers speak about structures and open structure. Okwui speaks about many futures for the world. I think we are going to break down the walls and have more interaction to become an open book. I am writing, but I feel I have nothing to say; therefore, I need to meet people to open the debate... open structures... my pavilion will be open to the public, open to anybody who has questions or answers.

NOBODY IS ANYBODY / THE BODY / BODY LANGUAGE / BODY DRAMA / NEW BODIES / BODY BUILDING / BUILDING A BODY...

A SPACE / A ROOM / A SALON / A STUDIOLO / A GALLERY / A MEETING POINT / A SALON / A DIGITAL PLATFORM / THE ROOM...

SPACE IS HOME / HOME-LESS BECOMES SPACE-LESS / WE THINK NON SPACES / WE LIVE IN NON SPACES / WE LIVE...

SHELTERS

PLATFORMS

GATHERING

PAVILIONS

BEGINNINGS

CONNECTING

SAUNA

SETTINGS

NOSTALGIA

Nostalgia is a nice word to write about because the concept of the past is always chasing me just behind my shoulder. I don't like to look back and when I do I feel sad. The past for me is synonymous with old. It's as if the past was uninteresting. I had the same feeling when I was working in the archives of the fashion museum, MoMu, in Antwerp. I felt that the garments had to be brought to life instead of lying in a drawer or hanging under white canvas waiting to be discovered by a researcher, or waiting to be seen in an exhibition. This lead to an idea for styling that came to life working together with Akiko Murata, a student from the Antwerp Academy in one of our exhibitions, *Backstage II*. We created a collage of contemporary fashion garments mixed with archive pieces, respecting of course the rules of conservation. We treated the garments, hats, gloves, scarfs with care, wearing our white gloves, overlapping them or mixing them with an A.F. Vandevorst, a Prada jacket or a crinoline, playing with the silhouette. It gave us great satisfaction! As a director of the museum I could take the risk, but I can imagine that it would have been impossible in a very respectable fashion museum in London or New York. Tricking the audience about time and memory gave me great satisfaction and provoked a therapeutic effect. I sometimes feel that nostalgia is the enemy of innovation, but when Tilda Swinton smelled the perfume of a garment during her performance of *The Impossible Wardrobe* at Palais de Tokyo created by curator and performer Olivier Saillard, time and space overlapped entirely in the odour of the person's jacket. This memory creates a nostalgic but positive feeling, as if the owner of the garment was present, standing between us. We can smell his presence; smell and touch powerfully evoke nostalgia; I can feel his touch or his kiss... I can imagine how it was being together... I can see her dying again and again, I saw his last breath leaving his body just before dying. Death is surely linked to this moment. There were many of those moments in my life, seeing my mother-in-law, my mother, and my father die, and my dearest friend Christine too. Those are important moments for reflection to understand your own life and happiness, the relativity of our time in this world. Nostalgia takes over when we listen to the songs of Leonard Cohen and it is inevitable that the words, the rhythm of the music and his voice will bring back a lot of memories! In fashion nostalgia is the worst of inspirations; the brains stops working when we step back into our childhood and to the memories of our grandparents and parents, fabrics become grey and dusty, colours sad and the silhouette long and romantic, but if Sissel Tolaas, the aroma artist, makes a scent related to emotional memories, then I feel nostalgia is a welcoming moment to step into the future. For myself, I discovered that I use a daily perfume that is not related to nostalgia. I rarely use perfumes with a smell of nostalgia and when I do I think they are not suited to my body and my mind.

The decision of Renzo Rosso, CEO of Diesel, to nominate Mr Galliano as designer for the haute couture collections of Maison Martin Margiela drew attention to the brand again and therefore is in itself a success. Commenting on this fact is irrelevant; discussions about whether Mr Galliano deserves a second chance or not is not my main preoccupation and concern. The protagonists of the brand have disappeared, exhausted by trying to keep their integrity. The discussion is therefore based on how the fashion system should evolve and why Renzo Rosso was not able to find a younger designer — fresh, contemporary with a less dramatic aura around him than John Galliano. The aim of this appointment is linked too much to the visibility that Maison Martin Margiela needs at the moment because its collections today are bad imitations of the basic and iconic elements of the house; the fabrics and ideas are poor replicas of what they once were and it seems nobody can tap into the essence of the style and tailoring Martin so brilliantly conceived. I would like to examine the meaning of the term 'Haute Couture' and find out if tailoring is still the main goal of this sphere, where more young designers are coming on the scene but do not always respect the high standards of luxury, beauty and elegance that 'Haute Couture' should embody. It should be a laboratory of ideas for designers where they could have time to study new techniques, patterns and body shapes and fabrics that reflect the new technologies and show the way to the future of the fashion system. 'Haute Couture' should become a laboratory, an institute that is accessible to designers, artists, researchers, architects, scientists and curators where they can experiment and design a new world, discuss and debate with buyers, retailers, consumers to re-design a sector that is losing itself in an increasingly frenetic rhythm where the collections are not very interesting and exhaust all the people involved. It becomes embarrassing to see what a low ebb creativity is at today despite so many fashion schools and programmes delivering highly educated designers capable of turning the fashion system into a more interesting field; some companies are concerned by the disappearance of the generation of craftsmen and women; they should study the phenomenon of the dying dream of the fashion designer, the individual who is the creative brain behind a name. This is what I think following the nomination today of John Galliano and his come-back as a designer for a label and name that changed the history of Fashion — not with a theatrical approach — but on the contrary, with a concept that was humble, honest, emotionally powerful but most of all intellectually rich.

FASHION IS UNIVERSAL / WE ALL DRESS / TO DRESS IS A UNIVERSAL ACT / SEEKING FOR IDENTITY OR SEEKING TO HIDE / COVERING FEAR OR COVERING SHYNESS / COVERING A BODY OR SHOWING NAKED FEELINGS / DESTROYING THE NEW / INVENTING THE NEW / WE DESTROY / WE INVENT / WE ARE BUSY CREATING AND DESTROYING...

THE PERFORMANCE / THE ALIENATION OF THE WORLD CREATED BY THE DESIGNER / THE MAGIC / THE CATWALK IS A WALK / WALKING TO THE FUTURE OR TO THE END OF THE WORLD FOR CONSUMING / LUXURY...

DEFINE THE HEROIC INCARNATION OF WHAT WE WEAR / THE DESIGNER / THE HEROIC WEARER / THE LOGO SNEAKER / THE LOGO / ANONYMITY IS THE FUTURE / OR MAYBE NOT...

IT'S SO GREAT TO BE UNFAITHFUL / I AM FAITHFUL TO MY DESIGNERS / I WEAR THEM / I KEEP THEM AND I LOVE THEM / MORE TO SAY / NO...

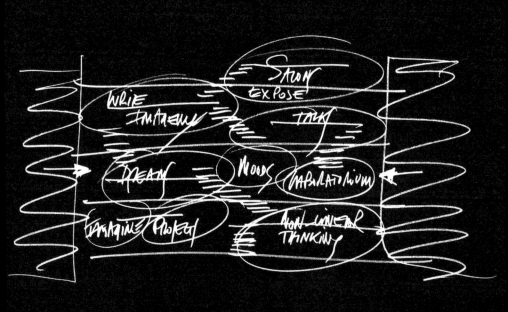

...ve known Linda for around ten years. I remember we had both recently moved to Florence. She arrived before me, and her ways aided my decision during a difficult moment in my life. I believe that living in different cities gives you a wider perspective and that distance gives you a clearer vision. To cut is to think, to quote Germano Celant. Cities appear to you like a great love at first, then they turn out to be full of flaws, and you cannot do anything but move elsewhere. Linda has something to argue about Antwerp and I about Rimini: the ancient Roman city and Fellini's magnificent theatre, a place very much about divertissement and little about fun, at least for me. We both think of Florence as a brilliant city that often misses its engagement with the contemporary. We want to do our part to make it a living, modern place capable of going beyond solely preserving its treasures. We love Florence, but people also need challenges, to make mistakes, to dream beautiful nightmares, to create monsters that drive the history of the future. In doing so, anger is often the lever, and restlessness is always there. We feel the need for change. We need a change because what might appear repulsive today could become the beauty of tomorrow. What we need here is a new Renaissance. We wrote it in *Momenting The Memento* and showed it in *Moments*. Therefore, I think that my connection to Linda cannot be measured in years and number of things we have done, but in community of intentions. To invent another word, we can measure it in 'light visions', meaning, as forward or inward as one's thoughts and feelings can go.

I still remember when we first entered Villa Favard and I told Linda that I wanted to paint everything white and get rid of the frescoes. She gave me a dirty look but shone with admiration at the audacity of such wickedness. It was a way of saying that the future can help the past, not just vice versa. In every chapter of this book, in the past recounted by Linda, I see the future of my 11-year-old daughter, all the artistic visits each summer...

travelling just the two of us around Europe, as well as the history lessons that I give her in private. Sofia is the future, and the future helps the past exist by giving it complete meaning. My idea is to look at the pasts that never became futures and to produce futures with no pasts to justify their existence. This creates space for possibilities and the possible space for creativity. Fathers are the mothers of today; we are full of scars, fierce and fragile. Yet Linda taught me that the aggressiveness of those who cause pain stems from their weakness. They are often the same people that do not understand that art, fashion and all forms of creative expression are necessary. This is, in essence, what differentiates us from animals and prevents us from being beasts. Like art, fashion is a question of identity, it forces us to look in the mirror, to watch others and make them look at us. We are all archetypes of something deeper, but it is among the others that the expression of our identity is denied or expressed. This simple concept was also the basis of the experimental method born with Fashion Brand Management, the beginning of my true career. It was a vision of the future that guided us and kept criticism behind us. Instead, it is important to think big and look forward, as long-term vision is the condition needed to make sense of every short-term decision. We have no more time to do anything. Yet they say history is over. Perhaps the world we live in is too fast. Is fashion nowadays too fast? Yes, but life also takes time to flow and once you stop, everything seems to have happened in a moment. In the same way, the whole, the essence of things, can be concentrated into a moment. It is only a matter of eliminating the superfluous. Life takes us one way on paper, but we often end up being and doing something else, something unexpected. When I finished university, I was offered to stay as a researcher, but I refused in order to make music. From there I moved to fashion and am now in school again, where I was meant to be since the beginning. Crazy, isn't it? Life is a vortex, as the title of this book states and is neither slow nor fast. My public life has little weight compared to Linda's. This book addresses fashion from the perspective of a giant that has interpreted it throughout time. Antwerp Six? Yes, but not only that. Fashion has the bad habit of labelling, hence the need for 'non-fashion fashion'. This is a key to reading fashion that we maintained even after

Linda handed me the baton to Polimoda's management. Education is the only place where it is possible to experiment; it is in younger selves that there can be a new beginning, thus it must be pursued assiduously. And every time the students leave, we cry. Perhaps because with them leaves a new beginning. The work of the educator is very difficult. If you believe in it, you must accept giving everything without receiving anything in return. Nonetheless, I believe that the insight of my generation is particularly important for those in their twenties. The forty year olds of today have lived in two completely different worlds: before and after the fall of the Berlin Wall, before and after the internet, before and after globalization. And we experienced all these changes on our shoulders, with the precariousness of work, growing illiteracy, the crisis of shared social values and changes in spatio-temporal parameters, the body, imagination and the concept of truth. It is an unrecognisable world compared to what we experienced at twenty years old. Students must know. This is also why we stay in school: to teach life, not only skills.

This book is raw, simple, direct, rough and sweet, sharp and inspired, like a child's story. There is no room for mediocrity. Linda did not want to write it, but she did well to do so. As she herself says, 'Our blood is red, but can turn black; it never turns white'. So, at some point it is important to put things in black and white. Linda was a very important person for me: we got drunk, invented courses, wrote books, launched slogans, organised events, smiled, cried, swore and rejoiced, a real sliding door [moment] for me. Coincidences happen. In the light of the years that have passed thus far, I can say that she has been my mentor, and I hope that with this book, in a small way, she may also be yours.

Danilo Venturi
23.01.2019
04:15am

MIRROR

We never observe what we see. We never like what we see. We always try to see differently. We speak to the mirror and we catch a fragment of who we are. We see an effigy of ourselves or a fragment of what we think we are in the mirror. We can imagine another vision of what we see. We can be blindfolded but still see ourselves. We can be shocked or saddened by what we see. If fashion is the mirror of society then we have a problem. Society doesn't look good and nor does fashion. Bodies are covered by tattoos not by clothes; faces are changed by syringes, not by beautiful make-up. Shoes are uncomfortable to walk in and garments are too expensive for everyday wear. We have the same love-hate relationship with the mirror as we have with fashion. The mirror gives us an effigy of what we are, it speaks the truth about ourselves, which is why we search for self-confirmation. Are we searching for new aesthetics, or new ethics? We need to decide. We need to measure ourselves against what we see and this is not so nice. The mirror doesn't lie. On the one hand we see this tribal freedom of expression or the absence of predefined codes. We are free to dress, to speak, to shout what we think. But it is still a very conservative world out there! I have not yet screamed in anger at the way tourists dress in a city like Florence (we are not on the beach, guys! So please, wear a decent dress or shirt!). We are hypocrites constantly lying to the people we pass in the street. And when we do happen to speak the truth, it feels shockingly arrogant. There are many reasons for looking in the mirror and speaking to ourselves as if we were going to confession with a priest and it might be good once in a while to criticise myself about some arrogant behaviour. Maybe looking in the mirror for longer helps. Now I see only an aging woman, sometimes tired, sometimes full of energy. I never liked my appearance, I always thought my face was too round, my hair too dark, my body too fat, my legs ok but only with stockings, my belly too plump… acceptance is a great quality! The mirror is a metaphor for what we hope to see, beauty… and therefore we need to analyse ugliness. Remember Beauty and the Beast; I like the beast because I am attracted by his strength, overwhelming greatness and romanticism. He, the beast, is male and he is fragile and tender. That's why ugliness is also tender, and reflects beauty.

The Belgians

Inspired by The Absence of Work: Marcel Broodthaers, 1964–1976, *by Rachel Haidu, associate Professor in the Department of Art and Art History and the Graduate Program in Visual and Cultural Studies at the University of Rochester. Belgianness; following Baudelaire's conception of 'Le Belge' we could speak about 'Lenteur belge. / La Paresse des Belges.' Laziness signifies the Belgian insolubility within the fluid, 'equal and convertible' relationship between the two terms (multitude and solitude) that constitute the poet's pleasure. Page 19 and page 20 It seems that work is not absent but just unseen, like an invisible message.*

Those invisible messages are the most inspiring for people to catch. We can translate the invisible into the tangible and in doing so discover what to neglect, to delete, to avoid. By deleting we can find the truth. The truth as such is again invisible, but it is recognisable to others. This is what is happening when a new didactic method is based on facets of different invisible truths. The different pieces form a whole, a body of concept-based research, analysing the existing facts, then by deduction and by creative thinking finding a key for the future. Is this methodology viable in a society based on economic success? Yes, it is. We search for the unknown in ourselves and in others. We try to discover why we are as we are and why others did what they did. Why did they paint, travel, write books, analyse or criticise? Why did they provoke, or transform their work by pushing the limits? To make a better world, and to avoid falling into the easy trap of mediocrity? We cannot follow a path that does not challenge us to do better. Always better... always better... this search for quality is difficult in an ever more complex world where cultures overlap, different values and languages overlap and float around one another. We speak all languages badly, we try to understand each other, but do we succeed? We apparently live in a more global world but it is absolutely time to start thinking and understanding each other's ways of life and ambitions. And education is key to bringing us together into the dialogue to reveal the invisible.

CURATE / WHAT / HOW / CURATE / CURATE AN OBJECT / CURATE
YOUR BRAIN / CURATE / THE KITCHEN TABLE / THE DREAM /
CURATE / THE DRESS / THE BODY / THE SPACE / CURATE...

I AM A CURATOR, A TEACHER / A DREAMER / A CRITIC / A DISRUPTOR
/ A WOMAN / A MANAGER / A CONNECTOR / A TUTOR / A WIFE / A
BUILDER / A WRITER / A DAMNNN DISTURBER...

VOICES / I HEAR VOICES / SCREAMING / ATTACKING / SEDUCING /
DESTROYING / EMBRACING / SILENCE ...

...30 / 40 / 50 / 60 / 70 / AND THEN... MORE...

A VORTEX
TRANSITION
BIRTH
CITY
A JOURNEY
DISCOVERING
THINKING
TWO
A BEGINNING
CUT & THINK
LIVING
SUCCESS
INCOMPATIBLE
SPACE
FLUIDITY
LOVE
LOOKING
INSPIRED BY
ARCHITECT
TRANSITION

Curating in the Loft

We put garments on the floor; I have this habit... I can see things better when they are lying on the floor. Not only students' work, but Comme des Garçons garments, drawings, patterns — all were presented on my concrete floor. Press, buyers, friends came to see the garments of CDG that lay there as objects because of the interesting patterns... it's hard to explain that, from a two-dimensional pattern, you dress a three-dimensional body. The two-dimensional perspective of the clothes pattern is an interesting subject studied by Janet Arnold, Rei Kawakubo and many others. I curated an exhibition at MoMu in Antwerp, on patterns. Two-dimensional patterns were exhibited flat alongside the made-up garment on a dummy to show the results of the creative form.

Curating Geometry

I was nominated in 1998 as the director of the newly born Antwerp MoMu Fashion Museum. The museum was the continuation of the existing Textile and Costume Museum Vrieselhof. I imagine I must have impressed the deputy of Culture of the Antwerp Region with my innovative ideas of management and exhibition policy. The idea of adding contemporary designers to the existing costume and lace collection was a great innovation for the quite traditional costume museums worldwide. My priority in that first year as a museum director went to the archives, photographing every object, re-organising them and preparing the digitalisation for the move to the new ModeNatie building; the newly bought compact storage systems would soon become their new home. But in the meantime, awaiting the opening of MoMu, I was slowly attracted by the idea of curating my first exhibition in the city of Antwerp itself; as the museum was still under scaffolding I went on a quest around the local museums of the Sint-Andries district looking for exhibition spaces there. I started drawing the geometrical shapes on a sheet of paper but could not imagine how to present the garments in the historical or contemporary spaces that were available;

and then I met Bob Verhelst. He worked in Rome for theatre and museums and immediately we started to collaborate on the scenography. Bob also worked for Maison Martin Margiela in Paris and we had known each other since the Academy years. Bob added more locations and finally we ended up with seven: Vleeshuis Museum, Museum of Ethnography, Museum Plantin Moretus, Pieter Paul Rubens house and museum, the Muhka – Museum for Contemporary Arts, the Sint-Andries church and finally the Royal Museum for Fine Arts. An amazing range of different locations selected for their different historical and cultural sensibilities and matching the concept of the geometrical shapes I designed on my piece of paper. The match was perfect.

Bob and I decided to start working defining the themes by locations. The theme of 'wrapping' found its destination in the Vleeshuis building. At the beginning of the 16th century, the Duke gave permission to build a new meat market. It was fully paid for by the butcher's guild and was twice the size of the previous building. The basement of the building had a very simple shape — just a large rectangular floor. We also found the concept of wrapping was present in the spiral staircase of the building. Bob started to select the garments, and here we ended up with several pieces by Belgian designers such as Maison Martin Margiela, Ann Demeulemeester, Dries Van Noten, Walter Van Beirendonck and A.F. Vandevorst. We added a wrap felt coat of Angelo Figus, a graduate of the Antwerp Academy, and a pattern of Madeleine Vionnet based on wrapping. The curating had started well.

In the Ethnography Museum, we were inspired by the collection of the non-western cult objects from Africa, Asia, America and Oceania. Here we mostly studied the volumes of two-dimensional garments related to the fabric and the body. We investigated the relationship between the body and the amount of material used, the fitting and the measuring. We documented the geometric measurements to show the volume of caftans for men, like the 'Tibbi' which we exhibited together with a two-dimensional shirt of Walter Van Beirendonck; a child's shirt from Gayo in Indonesia, was exhibited with its measurements next to the two-dimensional hall pattern of Caroline Lerch, who had just graduated from the Academy. A light grey transparent caftan from Veronique Branquinho's 1999 collection and a cape of Raf Simons from our archive at MoMu were some highlights in the Ethnography museum.

The first printing and publishing house of the Plantin and Moretus family became our next location. Christophe Plantin spent his life among books. Together with his wife and five daughters, he lived in an imposing property on Vrijdagmarkt. The printing company was founded in the 16th century by Christoph Plantin, a major figure in contemporary printing with an interest in humanism; after Plantin's death it was owned by his son-in-law Jan Moretus. As a child, I visited the Museum many times and had always great respect for what the Plantin family had created 450 years ago. It was obvious to Bob and me that folded and pleated garments were at home in this great location with the garden and the tranquillity of so long ago, inspired by the folding of the quires of the printing studio. Our most prestigious piece was a pleated garment of Rei Kawakubo in the archive of Comme des Garçons from the collection *Clustering Beauty*, summer 1998; it arrived by Art Transport from Japan to be exhibited in this magic location! How did Bob organise this? One day, I need to ask him for all the details. A pleated and folded dress of Junya Watanabe from the collection *Object* came to Antwerp from the same archive. Loan agreements, transport costs, designers' confidence — it all worked perfectly like planned.

We continued to fill in all the spaces we had chosen. The Sint-Andries church was the most enigmatic for me, but Bob designed a stage where we exhibited the garments on special supports he created; we selected patterns and garments inspired by circles, as the concept of geometry was approached from a symbolic angle that underlined the round spiritual, metaphorical and allegorical significance of the circle. A shoe design of Bruno Pieters was based on the circular pattern, a Chinese skirt from the Miao people in the Guizhou region, and a skirt from a Zulu married woman in South Africa — all private loans — were amazing objects, frage garments that Bob found the perfect way and support to exhibit. We juxtaposed a green circle skirt by Bernhard Willhelm, who was of course the right contemporary designer to select for this thematic exhibition, and a crinoline from our own MoMu archive couldn't be absent. A red 1863 velvet cloak from the Sint-Andries church archives was exhibited on the floor before the altar. Slowly the exhibition came to life; magical moments of joy and satisfaction were almost minimised by the tensions provoked by this new experience. It seemed as we were about to achieve our goal.

Being given a room for our exhibition in the Rubenshuis, the house of the magnificent painter from Antwerp, was a great satisfaction. We divided the room into two parts with a diagonal wall as we wanted to create a dialogue between the one hundred pieces of the puzzle of Angelo Figus' garment *Arlecchino* from his 1999 *Cuore di Cane* collection and the *4 mouchoirs* of Madeleine Vionnet. Complexity versus simplicity. The dress designed by Madame Vionnet in 1918 arrived in Antwerp from the Patrizia Canino archive in Paris by International Art transport, accompanied by Lydia Kamitsis curator of the Parisian Musée des arts décoratifs! I had tears in my eyes when the box was opened and we saw the dress lying there ready to be carefully lifted out with white gloves and placed on the mannequin.

For every new location, we had to invent a new scenography. That's what makes curating 'in situ' so exciting! Especially in the Museum of Contemporary Art — the MuHKA — we planned a drapery workshop in which the audience, visiting the museum, could follow the birth of a garment starting from a piece of cloth with a geometrical form thanks to drapery techniques. The late Hieron Pessers guided in silence this workshop in the MuHKA with the students of the Royal Academy of Fashion Design.

Finally, we were privileged to be given a space at the entrance hall of the Royal Museum of Fine Arts, KMSKA. This prestigious museum hosting Antwerp-born painters like Pieter Paul Rubens and Anthony Van Dyck was closing the circle, it was the culmination of the exhibition. Our search for geometrical shapes and patterns concluded in a broader idea of creativity. How could we not be inspired by the grandeur and impact of the museum and by two of the most magnificent painters known internationally for their paintings hanging in the world's most famous palaces and museums. A wooden top and skirt by the designer Yohji Yamamoto, a loan of Harry Houben and Silvie, represented the infinite striving of designers to innovate. The wooden eggheads of the British designer Hussein Chalayan would have been nice juxtaposed with a portrait of Van Dyck, but this might be an idea for another exhibition that one day we will be able to design.

Bob made a catalogue of this very brief, one-month exhibition and so saved it from being forgotten for ever. Suddenly to our delight from Paris, a bus with curators, museum directors and journalists arrived in Antwerp to visit our exhibition. What an impact this exhibition would have made if we had had Instagram, social media, a team of digital communication specialists and iPhones to photograph all the installations to promote our curatorial moments...

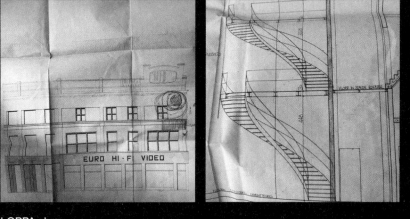

LOPPA shop
building Huidevettersstraat Antwerp
Architect Kris Mijs

LOPPA shop
building Huidevettersstraat Antwerp
Architect Kris Mijs

Curating in My Shops

Shopping experiences have changed over the years. After the doorbell situation where private clients entered to order a suit or a dress made to measure, windows provided an attraction and built a bridge between the client and the tailor or the fashion house. From window dressers to visual merchandisers the job of the 'curator' to attract the consumer (the doorbell ringer) and then move through to the act of buying has a long history. Nowadays the window is disappearing again and is giving way to a more mysterious or sophisticated discovery of the shop and the shopping experience. Sometimes display is reduced to the vulgar showing off of male bodies to seduce young girls and boys (see Abercrombie & Fitch). From dresses hanging like empty bodies on nylon strings to mannequins like the Japanese model 'Sayoko' that I ordered for my Quellinstraat store in Antwerp at the beginning of the 1980s from Adel Rootstein, the dress has to be shown on a fake body. Even today dresses look terribly sad in glass museum cases. Temporary exhibitions like *The Glamour of Italian Fashion* which I recently visited in London are disappointing. The dresses looked old-fashioned and not at all glamorous because both the choice of mannequins and the curating were disappointing. My point is that curating a window is an important exercise; sometimes you have huge windows, sometimes not; sometimes you have interesting light architecture, sometimes not; or the reflection might be terrible and the window only looks attractive at night or maybe it reflects the window of your competitor on the other side of the street or, worst of all, your window dresser is absolutely unaware of the message the garment could express. So when I opened my second shop I put the figure of the Laocoön, left forgotten in the basement of the Royal Academy of Fine Arts in Antwerp, in the window! Shame on me.

Curating in F20

Here I am, living and working in Florence. Now I have to build bridges in the footsteps of Arnolfo di Cambio, I have to write in the footsteps of Dante, I have to dream in the footsteps of Leonardo, I have to re-define the body in the footsteps of Michelangelo Buonarroti and I have to look at dress and dress codes in the footsteps of Eleonora di Toledo. Finally, I am looking at the stars like Galileo Galilei. For many centuries Florence was a creative centre; intellectuals, artists, politicians working in Florence were overlapping techniques of architecture, urbanism, decoration and craft creating the most intense moments in history and the most interesting projects, examples for the future hybrid world we are living in. A visual language was developed based on humanistic thinking where mankind stood central. Cultural interests were discussed in the 'salon', a gathering of artists and politicians during the Renaissance in Florence. Polimoda, member of IFFTI foundation, candidated itself for organising the annual conference in 2015 inviting 65 institutes having design and business courses in their didactic offer. When we received the agreement for organising the conference I started to implement what was so strongly already imbedded in my mood and personal mood board.

It was just before Christmas 2011. Danilo, Aki and I were talking about the future, about Florence, about our dreams and how to stimulate young generations. I had just returned from a trip to London where I had visited the exhibition *Postmodernism: Style & Subversion 1970–1990. Moment.* I put these books on the table: *The Medium is the Message* by Marshall McLuhan, Hans Ulrich Obrist's *Conversations* and *Postmodernism*, *Renaissance Florence* by Gene Brucker; we discussed and I drew a circle on the floor. I said, 'That's us, in the circle'; we have to connect with other educators, students and friends, opinion leaders, philosophers, architects; the city of Florence is the right place to meet, to connect. The re-birth started; a re-birth more centred around and about ourselves than about the city. (I discovered this fact one year later, after all the exhibitions, debates, parties and mails and huggings were gone). But this is not of a great importance.

Then it all started — finding locations, Danilo Venturi wrote *Momenting the Memento*, I travelled to Jaipur proposing the concept, launching the idea that fashion has to be curated and that Florence is the perfect city to do so. Exhibitions are living performances and we have the obligation to use our city to bring people together to create exciting moments that are important for teaching and learning. What we achieved in May 2015 bringing together all those people coming from five continents, some we never met before, but only saw by Skype on our computer screen, became a long-time memory composed by teachers, artists, writers, philosophers, craftsmen. When they arrived in Florence the first day of the conference we felt that it was worth the suffering, the anxiety organising the event. We forgot the reason for bringing them to Florence because the success of the conference was now in their hands, not in ours. They had to connect to the six themes we created and to our six heroes, monsters, of the past with names as Dante Alighieri or Michelangelo Buonarroti. All this was only an excuse to bring to life a concept or a statement for all of us working in fashion education. Some teachers never experienced the creation of an installation and we guided them kindly thru their work, others were experienced but we had to adapt to translate their idea into a project. Things were said and slogans were written and unbelievable energy emerged; that was sufficient for us, the team working like hell to achieve these 'moments'. We created a bond between us because each of us contributed with our soul and with our passion and experiences. Will we be able to repeat those moments, now left in the files in our computers and printed in a catalogue?

We were orphans after the 'Momenting the Memento' conference. Tracy left Polimoda, Eva is searching, and finally Oleg changed his life and me, I moved to Paris with my husband. A chapter was closed. A work done. We were changed working on those moments, performances, events, parties; a drastically change of vision was resulting in a new future for each of us. We couldn't go on doing nothing of the same level of discussions and intensity of work.

what started as a think tank in Y20 became a radical change for all of us who intensely worked on the event. After 'Momenting the Memento' we dreamed other dreams, we spoke other words, we saw other spaces and we experienced a desolate void in our bodies. Who could have predicted this before the conference? Michel Maffesoli maybe analysing our dreams and ambitions, analysing a society in constant change.

Curating in Shop Windows

My job as a *sensei* was a very pleasant one. I could advise my students and in return I heard a lot of stories about their lives, their inspirations, their hopes or their fears. In Antwerp our methodology was and still is based on discovering yourself and expressing an attitude that emerges from re-search and quality, edited results. Presentations are important, whether to us — the faculty — or to jury members at the end of the four years of study. We invite jury members from the fashion world, experts, to join us in the fi-nal evaluation of the collections. Locations can be a warehouse, the base-ment of a languishing cultural centre, the city hall, or the building that later became the 'Modenatie'. We invented different kinds of connections with the city of Antwerp itself. One of the projects became 'Vitrine', as we called it; a walk from one shop window to another in the city's fashion centre. Many shops participated and from the initial twenty-five shops, the project ended up with 120 or more windows to present the models of Academy students. I repeated the idea in Florence, first in Via Tornabuoni and later in Via Maggio, the street of the antique dealers. In Via Tornabuoni we put a garment made by a young designer in the Hermès store. This was quite a shock! The same happened with the Roberto Cavalli window, the Max Mara entrance and the windows of Pucci, Ermenegildo Zegna and Salva-tore Ferragamo. Later, the experiment in Via Maggio was very interesting because it was so different and the antique dealers so prestigious. We created a dialogue with art, antique objects and drawings. I quite enjoyed convincing the antique dealers to participate. Some welcomed us very warmly, others were more conservative. The effect of both experiments

as to elevate the work of the students to a higher level. If the mannequins, the light and the window are interesting, and if there is a coheren
match between the design and the shop, then both situations benefit from
his encounter. Students and shop owners liked the confrontation but
was not able to repeat the project because it was too time consuming. The
final result has to be up to the standard of a designer fashion house and
reputation. Cities are labyrinths and you can use them in different ways
Just as you can lose yourself in the streets of Florence, you can lose yourself in the fashion system.

Curating in a Warehouse
(Antwerp '93, Cultural Capital of Europe)

A Flemish journalist chose the title 'A Stubborn Choice for Art' and the
New York Times 'What's doing in Antwerp'. In the 1990s fashion became
a cultural phenomenon that could be promoted as an Antwerp city attraction and it became what we now call a perfect subject for branding a city
Luckily, the first time we were able to present our work was when Ant
werp became Cultural Capital of Europe in 1993. Erik Antonis, the curato
or 'intendant', was an interesting person, understanding the meaning o
fashion in the cultural field. Previously administrator for a theatre compan
in the Netherlands, he was known for creating high quality programmes
We were invited to organise an exhibition with the Fashion Academy. The
budget was the smallest of all the events and was communicated late
because the programme was actually already defined and announced, bu
t was a great opportunity! We were allocated the Sint Felix warehouse
an empty warehouse near the port! I recall we had an exhibition showing
thirty years of the Royal Academy, thirty graduates showing their work in
an installation, an exhibition of the photography of Patrick Robyn and Ann
Demeulemeester, a photo exhibition of Dirk Bikkembergs, and a performance evening with 1000 slides representing the city of Antwerp by Dries
Van Noten and, in August, an event by Walter Van Beirendonck in the hal
of the warehouse. 30,000 visitors enjoyed the installations. No iPhones o

Pads… so we have no catalogue, no website, not one picture, hardly any interviews but only memories… I found just two articles; one of a journalist explaining the political scene in Antwerp at the time and another that appeared in the *New York Times* giving all the top reasons for visiting Antwerp Cultural Capital. Analysing both texts you can understand the culture and life of Antwerp in Europe in 1993.

Curating in a Museum
GenovanversaeviceversA and other exhibitions

We found a 11,000 square metres building in the middle of the city centre. Students were always looking for empty spaces where they could organise their installations. This building was located in an area called 'le Petit Paris' which architecturally was a kind of replica of Haussmann's Paris. The building was constructed at the end of the 19th century. We discovered archive pictures showing that the building had hosted a very chic hotel and on the ground floor was a shop called Old England. Later in the 20th century it housed the offices of the National Gas Company. When we visited the building some small folders were lying on the floor and I picked one up. So, to cut a long story short, the city of Antwerp gave us the building for a project that we called *ModeNatie*, a house for 'Fashion', for the Fashion Department of the Antwerp Academy and the Flanders Fashion Institute that I founded in 1996 together with Patrick De Muynck and Geert Bruloot. It was also to house a museum, shop or bookshop. A dream is a dream is a dream… but if you believe in the project sometimes it comes true. The mayor of Antwerp, the cultural attaché Hugo Schiltz, the minister of Economic Affairs Wivine Demeester, the governor of the Province of Antwerp, the Chamber of Commerce, private companies. So, unexpectedly I became the museum director of what we baptised the MoMu after presenting a museum management plan and vision to the Province, transforming a conservative historical fashion museum exhibiting 17th- to 19th-century dresses, hats, shawls, shoes and lace objects, into a contemporary Fashion Museum and Gallery. I started to study the ICOM rules and regulations of museum management so it would become an officially recognised museum and to understand the different objectives and rules for a museum in all its facets. The four cornerstones that a museum rests on are: Conservation/Presentation/Archiving/Education. A good friend of my husband and myself, Jan Debbaut, director of the Van Abbemuseum in Eindhoven saved me. With a few drinks of Belgian beer and many drawings on sheets of cardboard he gave me all the instructions for how to become a good museum director, respecting the rules of conservation, education and exhibition policies. I am still very grateful for his advice.

Curating Patterns

The fashion laboratory is the workshop where we design, sew, drape, talk, add, cut or stitch. We invent or re-invent a garment. We start from the basics of the pattern, the flat two-dimensional paper and from it create three dimensions in calico fabric. That non-colour helps us to concentrate purely on volumes. The crème colour is like an artist's canvas; we can write on it, we can pin or fold, we can put it on a mannequin or throw it away in anger. There is nothing like a philosophical debate, but there is a real struggle that only the designer and the pattern designer know. Why call it our laboratory? Because we invent new techniques, new shapes, new volumes or profiles. So far *Artistic Development in (Fashion) Design* by Clemens Thornquist is the only book that has succeeded in explaining this struggle. I have hundreds of books in my library, but none can be compared to this book written by Clemens Thornquist, published by The Textile Research Centre, CFT The Swedish School of Textiles, University of Boras Sweden

TO CUT IS TO THINK
GERMANO CELANT
LOOKING AT FASHION
BIENNALE FIRENZE 1996

The magical instance of the cut that makes the garment has thus passed through all the various thresholds of artistic creativity. The time has now come for fashion to decipher its latent forces and desires and recognise itself as a free and original discipline, knowing full well that art will never lose sight of it, but only continue to respond with cuts and critiques.

Germano Celant, Looking at Fashion, *Milan: Skira, 1998, page 36*

Meetings Artists

Meeting Joseph Beuys

In 1976 we were at the 37th Venice Biennale. Dirk interviewed Joseph Beuys. We stood around and followed him for a long time, waiting for the moment to approach him... he was walking outside the pavilion, it was during the press days and we had already filmed Michelangelo Pistoletto and many others. This interview was seen as very special. What can you ask an artist who is a strongly engaged person? I had just bought the Coyote book with the pictures where Beuys is in dialogue with the coyote. He signed my book... I never ask for signatures... it feels stupid, but this one was very important to me. In 1987 I visited Berlin. There was an exhibition of Joseph Beuys I will never forget. East / West / Wim Wenders / Mercedes Benz / Nick Cave / the bus to the exhibition / Immortal angels / Joseph Beuys / East / West... The Berlin Wall...

Joseph Beuys

für Linda Loppa

Venedig 16.7.76

Joseph Beuys   Coyote

Text und Photographie von Caroline Tisdall

Schirmer/Mosel

1976 Venice Biennale

Meeting Artists

Meeting Raf Simons

When I announced the closing of my Huidevettersstraat store and going into architecture or design, Walter Van Beirendonck said to me that a young guy called Raf Simons wanted to see me. So, there he was in my shop on the first floor and said it seems you are interested in furniture design and I want you as my promoter. Hey, this is a daring proposal! Well, yes, we can meet again, you can show me your designs and then we will see what we can do. Our next meeting was in the Loft, my home on Verlatstraat 12-14 in my 'kind of office' that I had created on the second floor under the roof. The furniture he created for his final year studies in Industrial Design at Hasselt in 1991 was amazing! There were seven cupboards; the Corset, the Butcher, the Burma, the Male Accessory, the Wire-netting, Chains and the Snake. The materials related in a way sometimes to fashion sometimes to garments, using leather, snake skin, wool fabric for the corset, or chains forming a protection. We started taking photographs, writing press releases, listing press contacts and thinking of eventual distributors. Finally we had some interesting contacts and press articles, for example in *Interni*, an Italian design magazine (July/August 1992). Raf's invitations were interesting, using the Belgian black/yellow/red colours; they were attractive at that moment in our brief history of Belgian fashion design. Raf gained experience in the furniture world, working for a furniture company, but he always came to watch the final fashion show of the Academy students. He was so obsessed by the energy emerging from the show, by the dreams and the studies that students had to translate into garments, their choice of music, the lighting, that finally he decided to launch his own collection making a few garments for the young boys he saw walking along the street on their way from college in their too small jackets because they had grown. My father helped him, explaining the basics for menswear tailoring and when he starting studying second-hand garments he found the key to his future career. His first showroom was in my home, the Loft. He was a designer at last! Although I thought that the garments were very small, he said that he was convinced about the sizing! And it worked so well on the friends who modelled for him, made his first video and photographs for his portfolio. A star was born! The Paris showroom had an atmosphere like the Andy Warhol Factory... his friends were there hanging around smoking or listening to music... very cool and a bit decadent, but different. This attracted the buyers and soon the collection was shown with amazing performances in Paris. A new chapter in the history of menswear was born as well as a friendship, lasting... lasting...

Meeting Angelo Figus

Angelo was sitting on a desk in the first year of the Fashion Department classroom. He was wearing a nice sweater, knitted in a special way; it attracted my attention. He smiled at me and later he confessed it was because of an interview I did on Italian TV that he decided to move and to study in Antwerp. It was a joy to see his collections and the themes he chose to express himself. The tailoring was extraordinary and from his first garment we knew we had somebody special in the department! His second year collection was menswear and was inspired by a guy who had been in a car crash! The garments were twisted and turned, but so elegantly made! His third year was the dream of a little girl sitting on the floor and looking at the sofa and the pieces of furniture in the home where she lived; the bed, the coffee jar, the blankets, the carpets, the ceiling; but it was the final year collection that made us cry! Angelo disappeared from school and I was a bit worried. Normally we met weekly with the students of the final year to discuss the evolution of their research. We would examine the first calico fragments of garments, we went through the first sketches and eventually fabrics. But Angelo was not there. One day he turned up and asked for a room with tables which he pushed together. I was surprised! And there on the table he spread out a work of art. It was all designed in a remarkable way! It was the story of his grandfather, a shepherd. Being Sardinian his attachment to the island is such a strong bond that this was more than a collection; it was the story of his life, his roots, his aesthetics, his attachment to the land! It was a masterpiece! Garments made in felt, padded with horsehair; the models were not professional, but ordinary people who walked slowly with stones tied to their feet expressing the memory of his Sardinian grandfather. The installation in the attic of the Royal Palace in Antwerp for his final year was astonishing! The dark rooms were ideal, each corner of the space hiding a surprise, and finally a naked man lying on a stone expressed the greatest suffering a person can bear to give his country. Milk, bread, water communicated a kind of religious sense, a magic contemplation of silence, reflection and sorrow. No words, only respect.

La figure emblématique de cette grande perspective c'est la figure mythique dans la mythologie grecque, de Prométhée. Prométhée, je le rappelle, c'est celui qui vole le feu aux Dieux et qui par là apprend à dominer la Terre. Prométhée c'est celui qui est actif, celui qui est performant, celui qui est fonctionnel.

Michel Maffesoli
Lecture Florence, March 2015

OPINION

The Factory talks... the factory works, the factory thinks, the factory moves, the factory walks, the factory posts, the factory makes, the factory is, the factory designs, the factory creates, the factory comments, the factory travels, the factory writes, the factory inspires, the factory speaks, the factory dreams, the factory meets, the factory visualises, the factory connect, the factory collect, the factory insist, the factory...

Stepping back is stepping forward; the distance becomes visible thanks to a heavy fog, all is vague, grey, non colour, non space, non existence, non work; the more the distance become distant the more feelings are become liberating, body and mind; dust, memories, knowledge, anger, joy. The more the dust goes away the more light is coming in. Light brings serenity, vision, and peace. Grey becomes black and white, becomes white, becomes contrasts and some colours appear but they very quickly fade away, because black is appearing and overrules. Black is strength, power and romance. Black is writing and screaming in the dark; black is a great colour. Black inspires and opens one's mind, because it gives a canvas to write on. Writing in white is delivering optimism and forward thinking. My white is absolute, a non-colour colour opening doors. The infinity of white is future and this future gives new prosperity. New is what we need, for making the dream come true and for recalling on inspiration. The horizons are grey, the water is black, the sun is white. Those layers of colours are resulting in layers of ideas, in layers of memories composed by black and white, like photography, they compose time. Cancelling colour means searching for essentials. Unnecessary colours are confusing us and confusing others; they have to be edited; we can look at the horizon and see colours; those are the colours we want to see in our imagination. The rainbow is black and white. Its different shades go from on point to another, fade away with the rain and the sun; they fight forming crystals who are becoming objects of desire. Nobody can draw colours without studying black and white. Shades, lines, shadows, bodies, light, deepening the flat surface are the artist's tools. He draws lines, searching for perspectives, bringing life to the object. The object starts to smile, to speak, to express emotions and thoughts; the three-dimensional is appearing and we must step backwards to look at the result. From a distance we see better, we can correct and understand our weaknesses. Coming closer is losing the perspective and vision but we can act and this is the utmost satisfaction; we can fight, we can look each other in the eyes. Close is dangerous because of losing control. We can feel the body, we can lose ourselves in memories; we give up the fight and blind ourselves in blackness. It's in the dark that we have clear visions, while sleeping we find solutions, we forgot a name and we find him in the dark; nights are days and days are nights; we work at night and dream during the day. Sometimes we lose ourselves in fear and anger; we become red, green or yellow; we are lost in pain and sorrow because colours are stressful. Most of the garments we wear are black or white; many blacks and many whites. We have to accept the colourless in our lives. We design in black or white. We think in black or white; we are black or white. Look at our skins, we have hundreds of coloured skins; the trend book of skins is the most interesting; from black to white we are coloured, starting from very dark ending in very white. We paint our face white; we never paint our face black. We absorb colour thanks to the sun and the sun gives us back our colour. Our blood is red, but can turn black; it never turns white.

Hello writer, it's a long time we met, actually we see each other daily bu are not connected. So let's start talking. Words are not necessary, let's use our body language, our eye contact, because we can express a thousand words. We spoke a lot in concepts, metaphors, commenting on luxury as such; not that we promoted poorness but essentialism, critical attitude panning out of the discussion our fellow companions because we were creating a new form of dialogue and vision. We couldn't always explain our thoughts based on anger living in a society who exploits creativity because of designers naivety… naivety and fragility. Designers are fragile and not aware of the grade of fragility and therefore ignore the fact. Instead of protecting them, more and more pressure has been put on their shoulders. *They Shoot Horses, Don't They? (directed by Sydney Pollack 1969 based on the 1935 novel of the same name by Horace McCoy)*. Who to blame… The consumer who wants more and wants it now, with a click on his iPad, or the dealer giving more and more creativity and thus create hunger for more. Internet is to blame but we all enjoy this fastness, don' we? We discuss it eagerly, translating the debate in our didactics while others promote knowledge based on theoretical practise. We won the battle! We won because we have followers, a generation of intellectuals who have hunger for the eventual solutions we offer them to think on, so they can put their vision immediately in practise entering companies withou fear. You motivated me to write. During conferences, invited as a guess lecturer I had to express those ideas before an audience mostly not aware of the fashion industry's challenges and evolutions and therefore I created slogans, put strong images aside, let them think while provoking, taking positions not always clear but at least challenging the audiences. No more fashion weeks or fashion weaks. Stop fashion weeks and then count them in days, weeks, hotels, travel expenses and final results. Meanwhile you at night wrote brilliantly a book or an e-mail saying loud what nobody eve could express so clearly. I spoke in public commenting your text and re iting it like poetry! Strong and sharp as a knife! Meanwhile I was thinking meanwhile you were writing, when I was writing you were speaking. I made my diagrams and you translated them into a poem. You put on paper those verbal trampoline tricks and I laughed and enjoyed them greatly! I put them on walls to underline the division between past and future and to create a context for garments and therefore for fashion. I curated your ideas. But suddenly the stream stopped; we were both at the end of this constant sharpness of the mind. We disagreed on details losing ourselves in games of power. We wanted to overrule the other and we started arguing on the context and the meaning of a word. Silence speaks. I gave in, tired of a useless game for power. I feel liberated now; writer… the Factory is writing and thanking you for the lost moments; the reality of the lost moments are sharper now and more precise and they make sense. The Factory has the strength to start a new cycle of talks. Are you ready, writer?

The Factory Talks… to Designers

Dear designers, how can we understand your search for creativity without putting you on a 'pied de stall'? We shouldn't care for you because you care about yourself. Surrounded by creative, lovers, promoters, press and photographers, models, muses, art directors, stylists you do well. You need their applause because it's stimulating your brain. You live on the borderline of your depressions or you live for arriving at deadlines in an always more complex society. More and more are you populating the globe and more creativity is needed. Less and less journalists are writing about you and buyers are not so many. So, you use Internet and e-commerce to survive. Your price setting is far too expensive because you only can produce small quantities and therefore you make second lines for improving your sales on whatever e-commerce possible. You teach here and there or sign contracts with famous sneaker companies; I hope they pay well for those little *capsule collections*, as they call them, because although they invest time and money in these projects, it creates a lot of visibility and credibility for the brand. Many of you compete for an award and this s good for your ego, if winning, losing is not a real problem but it might be embarrassing if you never win. Some of you are happy to work in a company learning a lot, keeping your eyes and ears open but mostly you quit after a while disappointed of how creativity is reduced to the minimum it's the complexity that makes the product, the endlessly research, every f today, we are more focused on product. Creativity is based on curiosity. To look at a painting, to read a book, to travel to exotic countries and confronting yourself in your subconscious with those experiences need time and money. I see you travelling a lot though because on Instagram and Facebook we see you in L.A., Tokyo, London, New York or on an island in the sun. Once in a while you disappear because you are working on prototypes or on new techniques using expensive fabrics, adding new print experiments and waiting for results from companies who give priority to famous names because quantities are more important and they have to be delivered soon. When you appear again in public it is hard to know how the business went; it is hard to ask how the results in the showrooms were and how buyers reacted. It's like asking how the relationship with your new lover is proceeding. It's a very personal question… and the answer will never be an honest one. So you talk about daffodils and the length of the sleeve instead of asking what is missing in your strategy, how is your cash flow situation and what is the best order so far in numbers? How many new shops represent your line and how many interviews you gave in the last few days? It's sometimes in the course of a chat in the streets or in a restaurant during a fast lunch you go further into the privacy of the designer's world. Do you appreciate those embarrassing moments when we come to congratulate you after the show? Mostly the atmosphere is great and even if the collection is not so good we hug and embrace you warmly. We can also avoid the embarrassing running up to the next show finding a cab and waiting for a friend for having lunch or dinner. How do you perceive us, the groupies? I am sure we are not priority. Press is priority, but maybe without us fashion life would be a bit boring and so you let us feel important maybe not sitting on the front row but at least being there to share the emotions and finally our friendship. What can we do to make your life more comfortable, although comfort is not helping creativy? Suffering is helping creativity. So, please designers, suffer and create beauty, elegance, and ugliness and let us dream with you. Embrace us instead of we embracing you! It will do no harm and we will feel closer to you. Finally, don't run away from the job as so many recently do because the system is rotten, but try to speak aloud and try to comment wisely on the impossibility to give quality to your work in this situation of pressure running constantly against time. Could you eventually work in team with different designers splitting the job in pre-collection, haute couture, social life, interviews, brand image and styling, photography and shows were sound, styling, imagery will be different? Mmm, indeed, it might create confusion and it seems not a good idea, sorry.

The Factory Talks… to Objects

Dear object, the Factory is going to try to work with you on Imagery. Can I be honest with you? I feel stylists, curators, and publishers, fashion film addicts and/or designers using or mis-using your identity and your reason for existence, sometimes mistreat you. I need to understand your history, the reason for being in this world and thus your utility linked on beauty, elegance or protection. I, the Factory, need to understand why you are lying in an archive or resting on a shelf in a studio or in a museum while your creator is absent, invisible and forgotten. The Factory is a judge and judges are not always right in their judgement, therefore I need to open the debate with you, the object, in order to rediscover your utility in this world. Objects can be objects of desire or repulsion, objects of suffering or enjoyment and lust. What can the factory do to bring you in the spotlight when forgotten in a library since ages and not be taken into consideration? Or do you prefer to lie there, forgotten and once in a while be taken in hand by a young pupil searching for knowledge? I can imagine it might be scary seeing suddenly the light and feeling hands surrounding your cover! But maybe you want to come in contact with other objects creating a dialogue, chatting like old ladies, about time and time management, about the long road you had to make for becoming an object or about the contact and relationship with your creators, sometimes many of them sometimes only one. Having five hundred years between you and another object the dialogue will be difficult; you will have to study the political and cultural environment of your wearer or user and understand the tribal components of the place you were created. Interesting though.

MOMENTS ARE MOMENTS OF EXTREME HAPPINESS / SADNESS / JOY / MOMENTS ARE REAL MOMENTS / MOMENTS ARE ABSENT...

CHALLENGE / INVITATIONS / CARS / DRIVERS / RAIN AND SUN / KISSES WITH FRIENDS, BUYERS AND JOURNALISTS / CRITICAL / AMAZED / EMOTIONS OR BOREDOM / FASHION / PLEASE GO ON...

CITIES / PARIS / ANTWERP / FLORENCE / ANTWERP / VENICE / FLORENCE / PARIS / INSPIRING CITIES / GIVING AND TAKING / STORIES TO TELL AND KNOWLEDGE TO SHARE...

Black/White

Conversations/Poetry

Pavilions/Rooms

Ethics/Aesthetics

Light/Sound

am on my first flight Paris-Florence, ending a chapter and starting a new one. I feel stronger, liberated and although shaken by the last months of my leadership as dean of Polimoda I feel very proud of myself and Dirk. We did it! We moved city, house, contacts, organised Internet connections, found new restaurants, saw our friends and found new ones, worked on the daily issues to resolve. My agenda is already pretty full of nice meetings such as a drink tomorrow at an exhibition in Lidewij Edelkoort studio, a visit to the video fashion film festival of Asvoff on Saturday or Sunday, a meeting with my new accountant, a coffee with Julie Gilhart, and a dinner with Olivier Saillard. The most important emotion is the fact that we belong in this apartment, our furniture is fitting in perfectly. Paris is like home, the food we waited for tastes better, the art experience we looked forward to in the Palais de Tokyo with the exhibition of John Giorno curated by Ugo Rondinone is rewarding, walking in the city, even with all the security and police around because of the recent terrorist attacks, gives a feeling of security and kindness. Strange, but after one day of moving and arranging our furniture in the apartment my Uber takes me to Charles de Gaulle airport for a meeting in Florence, and this is also an amazing experience. Reading today's mails creates a distance between my previous job and my new assignment and all seems strange already. I feel that finally I can work on priorities and be passionate again about my work.

While waiting in the airport I was thinking of *Chambre d'Amis*, an art project created and curated by Jan Hoet in 1986. Jan Hoet opened our minds thanks to his passion, his fantasies and his dreams. Many of us, art and fashion lovers, followed him in his craziness. Fifty-eight private houses hosted contemporary artists in Ghent, an event that became a milestone in art curating not only in Belgium but in the world. This project changed the perception of art exhibitions, or what a museum is or should be. He questioned the mission of the museum by bringing it into a private environment; artists, museum visitors, friends, art lovers, collectors were welcome

In those private houses. Ghent, a city always inspired by art and literature, was fortunate to have Jan Hoet as director of the Museum of Contemporary Art. Hoet was a man with a history, a survivor, a controversial person, a provocateur, a boxer and the son of a psychologist and a dentist. For three months, artists had to adapt and to disrupt private spaces; where daily life took place, the act of creation was reinvented by both the urban locations and artists interventions. Today we must be as creative, as inventive as Jan Hoet. With his example, he opened up unusual locations in cities, leaving the museum space to be what it is, with its stricter codes and cultural and educational purposes, while he stepped into new territories such as private houses, bridging private and public interests. His act, courage and belief in experimentation should be discussed and studied again to provoke non-linear thinking. Jan Hoet showed us how we can be transversal in our rational thinking: he opened up the area between history of art and contemporary artists, he opened up the dialogue between space and using space; he showed me how to use the transversal way of thinking; I thank Jan Hoet for what he did to open our minds and give us the courage to be brave and believe in what we do. I had the opportunity to meet him and thank him in the Museum of Herford. The exhibition – *(my private) Heroes* – was based on his desire to work on the image of the hero in art. Later he said that perhaps it was more a view on the anti-hero.

Chambres d'Amis must inspire us to bring fashion and fashion institutes together in a new dialogue to define the future of what we call the Fashion System. We can stage projects in 'non-spaces', locations based on the language of cultural expression, creating contrasts in the dialogue to stimulate creative thinking. From this a new network of creativity will evolve, able to find new solutions for the cultural and economic aspects of fashion. We can open a new field of education embracing fashion design, business and fashion art directing. In those 'non-spaces' we are freer to speak and to perform. We mould creative managers or managers who understand creativity; we will bring rational thinking alongside un-rational thinking. We must bring business to a better level of performance. Today brands who went public are scared to lose on the stock market, others are poored by Internet competition, others are scared to be scared... fear

...las to be erased and design students especially have to be guided in their search for authenticity and a professional approach.

Art is a driver that stimulates vision. An artist friend I met a few days ago said, I am not a contemporary artist; I cannot speak about my work or talk about the idea or the message behind my drawings, paintings, or videos. My work is seen in galleries or museum spaces and bought by friends but I am not contemporary. Strange observation. I analysed why she says this and am still intrigued why the distance between my attraction to art and a statement like this troubles me so much. Art is the expression of more than a nice picture on the wall. Art expresses a moment in society, or an opinion, a provocation or a personal journey, or it reflects the state of mind of a person or a generation. The John Giorno exhibition expresses a personal journey thanks to poetry and love encounters with artists such as Andy Warhol, and a personal diary, a photo album presenting old family pictures, articles and archives. The presentation by Rondinone, the lover and artist, the curating of his archives, and the filming of his *Thank You* show in black and white, all make the exhibition a performance, a memory and a timeline worthy of an 'Art Laboratory' such as the Palais de Tokyo. The spaces of Palais de Tokyo are 'non spaces', not defined, free for interpretation, not pretentious, not imposing anything, not stylish nor overwhelming. The artist, the curator, the poet, the performer is at ease. It is not guided or directed by a star curator or a famous museum director; different curators take risks, they question themselves and their artists creating new experiences at the Palais de Tokyo. Those experiences are lacking in today's fashion museums.

On my return from Florence after the Rick Owens show in Palais de Tokyo I called Danilo excited about the shows I had attended. The locations, the soundtracks, the collections were all in balance! It seemed to me that the wake-up call made by Raf Simons, Alber Elbaz and many others at the end of 2015 gave the avant-garde designers the right to be experimental again. But this was not the reason why I called him; I wanted to share with him my renewed enthusiasm for Fashion. I remember working on the IFFTI conference last year in 2015, avoiding the F word... It was used and overused. Its meaning was linked to figures and numbers and I felt that the passion for...

fashion was also gone and even commented on by the press, the buyers, the writers, the designers themselves. What was so positive about Paris Fashion week is that the Parisian calendar is a very good mix between the avant-garde and the established designer houses. I am not attending all the shows but I hope to be more varied in my chase for invitations. The excitement, the adrenaline and the emotion of being there, in the show, experiencing the scenography, the soundtrack, the community, the theatrical moment, the wait at the gate while photographers are taking pictures of the beautifully or badly dresses stars or the wannabe stars put me in a super good mood! Meeting friends, exchanging thoughts, commenting on the system, sharing future visions or projects, greeting the designer after the show, talking to friends you only see during fashion weeks but who are the friends we desperately need to continue our work with enthusiasm and passion whatever your job might be, organisers of fairs, buyers, press agents, famous stylists, architects, film directors, show designers, museum curators or perfumers, producers, artisans, weavers... This is the world I like but missed dramatically for a while. I am back in fashion and can use the word without hesitating or feeling bad because it means so much to me that I spend my entire life studying and sharing every single aspect of this business. A business that creates lots of jobs to the largest community of the creative class all over the world!

OPINION

My Book

My book is a living story written in fragments of memories, reflections, dreams, encounters, statements, put together as a collage. My book is not meant to start a debate or a confrontation; it is more a guide for understanding how creative people act and react. I need to talk about my life more as a clarification of my achievements and myself and how and why I acted as I did. My book is not based on philosophical research or historical facts but on what I experienced in moments that were important for me, why and how they define my next actions. I worked in teams mostly but I am a loner. This means that I take my decisions after talking and thinking a lot and mostly I am a bit absent. It means I am close to find solutions...

Timeline

The Carabaccia Table

A few steps up, at the left in the corner, there is the La Carabaccia table; it is situated in a corner, not hidden but not right in the attention of the other people present; we had so much fun at that table. Our choice in the menu always the same; *'una tagliata di manzo e una tagliata di pollo'*; with salad or potatoes. The spirit was always high at the Carabaccia table. Sometimes we were three, sometimes four and mostly two. The table inspired us; the subjects never prepared and conceptually interesting; strategies, dynamics were explored and the table reacted positively. It's like she liked our talks and stimulated the heaviness and the density or the craziness of the contents. We never prepared in advance those talks, it came like, a Carabaccia? Yes. At that particular table we commented on boring projects, we invented slogans for new courses, we created new words, we ignored the daily rhythm of the normal office meetings and talked nonsense; it didn't matter but it was always resulting in new methods for teaching or constructions and ideas for new projects, or exhibitions. The table enjoyed and stimulated our fantasies; she was at her best when we were sitting at her table and we were without bounds and without fear; I am sure the Carabaccia table needed a rest in the afternoon and was exhausted after our talks. But when in the evening guest were sitting at her she taught probably they were a bit boring. I am convinced our nonsense was more interesting than their stories about work and leisure; we stepped into the future without thinking of the consequences of our decisions or plans. After quite a few months, almost a year ignoring her, we stepped the three steps and turned to her and sat again at her table and I knew immediately she was happy. The energy was the same, the discussions good and constructive, the forward thinking great, the dialogue intense. The Carabaccia table recognized us and stimulated us again! The return to our desks was good; we knew we would implement one day the ideas we threw on the table. That Carabaccia table will hopefully be there forever because the people who were sitting and discussing while eating *'una tagliata di manzo e una tagliata di pollo'* will remember her as a real partner and an important part in our careers, in our friendships and our madness.

...ans is the third city I have lived in. Different cities influenced my life, Antwerp and Florence, but also Tokyo gave me confidence, and probably they offered to me the best moments — the most challenging to my knowledge and my intuition. Empathy is very important in Japan and think I had a lot of empathy with the Japanese culture. Although body language is very different, the cultural expression and understanding is very similar to my own state of mind. Therefore it is obvious that the brain is important but that intuition and free mental space are imperative for living in today's world. When I was hit by a van on a street in Tokyo I was in the hospital for three weeks with a broken hip; this was a real experience because even though I could not speak Japanese I could communicate with other patients in the hospital; my friend Take was a great help and the bond with Japanese culture became even stronger. When I worked a few months ago with Marialisa, Polimoda's librarian, on a project to choose thirty books in the context of the festivities for Polimoda's 30th anniversary, I went through the most significant acquisitions of books on design, designers' histories, fashion history, and we discovered we were at the end of different phases in the history of fashion and chapters in the history of acquisitions for fashion libraries. We also realised that we needed to start thinking of a new chapter. This was not a negative feeling but a relief. We felt that we were not really ready to think about what content or objects we should focus on buying for the archive, but we felt that this situation — instead of being stressful — was like a white page and thus very liberating. This freedom was a state of mind we had not experienced for a long time; we can launch new words in our vocabulary like... useless use the word so often today. I did so many useless projects in my life but they were the most rewarding. Is archiving useless? No, not at all, but we could eventually buy useless books for fashion, such as books on science mathematics, food or simply books on innovators in different fields and study their brain and vision. Showing archives is interesting to keep the...

...past alive and confirm our admiration for generations and techniques that have almost vanished. It helps us not to forget techniques we allowed to die because of industrialisation, because of economic and political changes, because of the speed of today's fashion consumerism. In museum scenography we mostly see a garment on a mannequin, read the caption that explains what we see, its origin, its technique, the eventual name of the wearer and the period in which the person was wearing the garment. When I opened the MoMu museum in Antwerp I refused to have captions. The visitor had to understand how to use their eyes, look at the garments and use their own imagination. Even the guides were supposed to be absent. I was not successful.

I visited three fashion exhibitions in one week where archives were used and re-used to comment on the garments and the wearers of the garments, analysing fashion and dress across many centuries. The first at the Musée des arts décoratifs in the Louvre with the title *Fashion Forwards*, the second at Musée Galliera, *Anatomie d'une collection*, and finally at the Metropolitan Museum in New York, *Manus x Machina*, based on technology in fashion. The Louvre shows 300 years of fashion, starting in the 18th century and clearly divided into the past and the future using two different scenographies. The historical context was provided by the interiors of the different periods and it looked all very inspiring. Interiors were cosy, romantic and aesthetically beautiful, and the painted landscapes were dreamy and soft. The contemporary history of fashion started in the 20th century and personally I would have placed the contemporary garments and silhouettes in traumatised landscapes, cities on the move in cold and dark environments to show disruption and decay. In the Musée Galliera the exhibition entitled *Anatomie d'une collection* shows garments worn by famous and ordinary people. Garments belong to us and we keep them sometimes for years in our wardrobe without wearing them because they have become friends. But I felt the garments lost their magic because they were less important than the person wearing them; my eye missed the beauty of the overall composition of the exhibition. The most intriguing section for me showed the simple garments worn by nurses, cooks, bakrs, shoe-makers just hung flat against the walls. For me those garments expressed the emotions the others were missing. Stories linking the designer of the dress to its wearer are fascinating material but the museum space is a static environment. The stories that described Olivier Saillard's performances with Tilda Swinton, or models and the shows of the 1980s are so emotionally strong that the museum space looks like a salon for a visitor interested in 'la petite histoire'. It is an exhibition I will visit again, to feel the link between owner and wearer better because on first impression this intimacy was missing. I am privileged to be part of the Advisory Council at the MoMa New York for the exhibition *Items: is fashion modern?* and therefore had to study the work of the architect Rudofsky. How will this exhibition evolve conceptually? Is fashion modern? Do 'modern' and 'modernism' have a positive connotation? Are we modern? But this is less important; thanks to the invitation, I have discovered a man, an architect, anthropologist, traveller, an art director as we call these people today. The *Items Abecedarium* presented at MoMa on Monday 16 May was an extremely interesting exercise with the 26 letters of the alphabet. In 2013 I completed a writing task based on 500 words relating to fashion using the alphabet as a guide. I was part of a project in which students of Trend Forecasting had to make an 'object'. Aki Choklat, course leader at the time, trapped me and thus I joined the group of students to make my object. I unrolled the 500 words printed on a paper roll and there was a great silence as everyone walked around to read the alphabet. Now I will do new projects on words, letters, diagrams writing concepts for non-linear thinking. My extensive knowledge and experience in fashion, whether it is education, curating, retail, branding, management or conceptual thinking, gives me a sense of fulfilment; being in the group of advisors in MoMa New York gives me great satisfaction. I am not a specialist in any one of those fields. Is that a problem? No, I am a happy person. I discover every day a new facet of myself, I can re-invent myself every year or two, I can advise in many fields. Now I am trying to write. A challenge!

In New York I visited the MET and I was happy again! Congratulations to Andrew Bolton with the exhibition *Manus x Machina*. Bright! Amazing pieces by bright designers very aesthetically displayed! The scenography by OMA work is well, the transparent canvasses show the structure built for the exhibition, and sound brings a nice context to the garments. My second highlight was the exhibition of Marcel Broodthaers at MoMa, my Belgian companion in art and absurdity, as I was able to catch the last day of his exhibition; a great homage to a poet becoming an artist, becoming a museum director, becoming an artist while writing, speaking, filming, curating, provoking a kind of naive reflection why we are so afraid of expressing ourselves today. His spontaneity inspired me and made me reflect on how I live today with the constant pressure of performing well. Perform, to perform, performing, form and perform. In all those words I will focus on form; maybe I am missing the form. Starting from form I will perform and search for a performance that will express my mood of the day. I will from now on write one word per day... my mood of the day. My first word of today is CLOUD.

HISTORY IS THE PAST / THE PAST IS THE FUTURE / THE FUTURE IS BECOMING HISTORY / HISTORIANS ARE THE PAST...

HISTORY IS GONE / THE PAST IS GONE / WHAT REMAINS IS FUTURE / WHAT REMAINS IS THE NEW THE NEVER SEEN THE AMAZING FEELING THAT ALL IS POSSIBLE / THE LONGING FOR THE NEW IS BASED ON CURIOSITY / BE CURIOUS / SEE WHAT BRINGS THE FUTURE WITHOUT THE PAST...

PASSION / WITHOUT PASSION NO FASHION / NO INNOVATION / IS INNOVATION THE KEY / THE KEY TO INNOVATE / TODAY NEEDS TOMORROW / WE NEED THE FUTURE / WE ARE THE FUTURE...

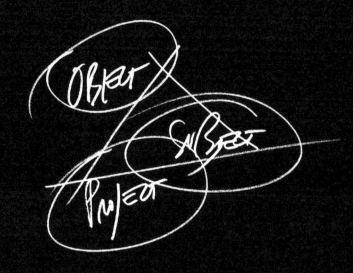

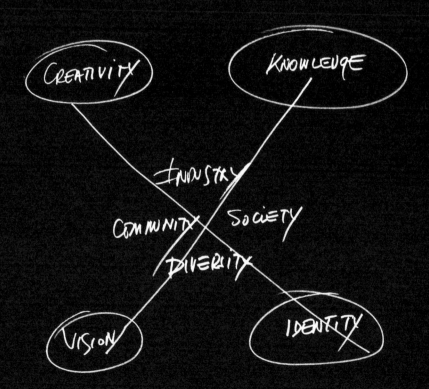

DON'T WAIT! TIME IS PRECIOUS / SHOW! SHOW! SHOW! / MANAGE CREATIVITY! / ART NEEDS CONCEPT, FASHION TO... / DREAM DURING THE DAY, WORK AT NIGHT... / CREATE! DON'T DESIGN... / EDUCATE... BE EDUCATED... / PATTERNS ARE PATTERNS OF LIFE / DRESS CODES ARE CODES... / QUESTIONING BEAUTY... ALWAYS... / BE SOPHISTICATED! / DREAMING IS REALIZING DREAMS... / WHAT IS PROGRESS FOR YOU? FOR ME IT IS THE WHITE PAGE / THINK NON-LINEAR... / LUXURY... SEND ME YOUR DEFINITION... / CIRCLES ARE ROUND... OR MAYBE NOT... / ADD THE THIRD DIMENSION, PLEASE! / BOMBERS ARE NO JACKETS... / SIMPLICITY IS COMPLEXITY... / GO TO THE ESSENCE OF THINGS... YOU WILL BE MORE HAPPY... / BE ANGRY! PERFORM BETTER!... / BAN UGLINESS... BAN VULGARITY... / WHERE IS THE DOOR NOBODY IS TAKING? / A LIFE IS MADE OF LAYERS... / PROPOSE, REACT! ACT! / BUY LESS BUY BETTER / BE FAST... SLOW DOWN / BE FOCUSED...

Michelle sends me some questions the day before the ABECEDARIUM presentation… here they are.

Dear Linda,

I hope you are enjoying a very good weekend! I just wanted to make sure you have the questions in advance of your interview tomorrow…
Warmest wishes,

Michelle

QUESTION 1: Is Fashion Modern? (And by this, we mean is current, contemporary fashion 'of its time'? Is fashion in step with contemporary society/culture? If yes, how so, and if not, why?)

Fashion has always been the antenna reflecting society. But since Internet we live in a liquid society and our values have changed. We cannot speak about one fashion as an expression of one society or one culture. Street culture is dominating and luxury has lost its authenticity. Shops are showcases and most of the buying is done on-line. Designer garments are rarely seen in the street and only a few brands are affordable and interesting to wear. I feel we are at the end of a chapter and this phenomenon is reflected in the many fashion exhibitions I recently visited because they are showing archive pieces as artefacts, but not as a dress code to be followed. Furthermore, seasons do not exist, gender is not an issue anymore and designers are reducing their shows, mixing both menswear and women's wear and changing the timing of their deliveries to consumers. Every single brand makes its own rules. This chaotic situation reflects society because it seems that we are in a transition. Until now we could read society by analysing the dress codes of the '50s, the '60s, the '70s, the

…'60s, the '80s, and the turn of the century. The book by Caroline Evans *Fashion at the Edge*, reflects the culture and the mood of the '90s very well. As I mentioned earlier, after analysing thirty years of books selected for the Polimoda library, the librarian and myself came to the conclusion we have come to the end of buying interesting books. It is as if a blank page was waiting to be written; after buying history books and pattern books in the '70s, in the '80s and '90s we bought books on designers and their styles, and with the turn of the century the books were on heritage and craft, then more recently we bought books on curating and exhibition policies, or related to marketing and philosophy. But now? What will we buy? We have to wait…

Art, architecture are experiencing the same sort of transition; do we feel the same lack of surprise? Can we still be surprised? Is technology the new force that is pushing us to new limits or have we already experienced it all? Zaha Hadid invented new spatial volumes thanks to technology and so did Frank Gehry, and Iris van Herpen for fashion, but what now? We are asking questions, we are in a moment of debate. The biennale of Venice and its curator Alejandro Aravena are also questioning what we build and what we have to build for future generations. Aravena says that architecture should improve people's quality of life and maybe this is the same for fashion, or let's call it 'Dress'. Let's look at the street. Tourism has taken over, tourists overrun cities, they dominate, and what we see is not a beautiful dress code. This question offers a chance to discuss the relationship between timelessness and temporality in fashion.

Secondary/sub questions might be how might you define fashion? Style? Modern? Contemporary?

Modern has always implied for me minimalism and essential volumes and styles. What I define as modern is a return to pure and conceptual thinking. But I feel this is a very personal interpretation. My definition of contemporary is 'non-existence' because 'today' is already old and what is yet to come is my challenge. So 'contemporary' has a 'temporary' conrotation. I think in a non-linear way and try to understand behaviour as a transcendence of different moments in history. Artists, the creative class as a society, do not work thinking of what is contemporary. They realise their dreams, and those are not linked to the moment of today. They are visionaries using intuition to create, to think, to write. Intuition is the new contemporary. It is based on knowing, and attitude combined with knowledge and curiosity.

Specifically, do you think fashion education for students today is equipping them for the current climate? How have you seen fashion education evolve over the three or four decades?

I feel education is in the same transition. Education systems are old. Luckily I had the chance not to teach but to have a dialogue instead, a conversation with my students. In fashion this is essential because the skills of a good designer are based on technique, tailoring and research. Fashion education became a business and only a few schools coach students to have a method for developing their personal vision and identity. Especially in fashion design, courses are becoming dated. A new laboratory should be created and the industry should be more involved in this new dialogue. A new kind of teacher should come into being drawing on psychology and real experiences in the field. I also feel the study of fashion should be diversified by inviting scientists, poets, painters... to debate creativity together.

QUESTION 2: What is the most critical/compelling facet of contemporary fashion today, and why? (e.g. think of intersectional issues, could be labour, politics, economics, gender, local vs. global, sustainability)

The most compelling facet of fashion today is the lack of critical attitude. In times of scarcity we are more creative, in times of war we use sustainable solutions, in political turmoil we get angry and we start a new movement. We are a new global society and we are starting to realise the potential of sharing knowledge, but we live in great luxury and we are not angry we are not motivated, we have fear, we doubt and have no leaders, we don't believe in our values, we are in a transition. For the moment we want to please, be charming but we feel that we are lacking honesty in our approach. We feel guilty, and therefore sustainability is a good topic. Of course we have to realise we are behaving badly, we have to find solutions, but fashion has the right to be unsustainable.

Secondary/sub question: how long have you felt this as a pressing/ urgent issue — is this very recent as a concern, or longstanding?

I am at my best when I am angry or better concerned. I find solutions when I feel bored with an existing situation. That's why today I feel motivated more than ever, pushing myself to reflect, to make diagrams for new methods of teaching, writing, curating. I am always in a state of thinking, searching, or trying to find a solution for a situation. I would like to change but am afraid I never will, and my team always knew that after the holiday period I would come back loaded with new ideas and projects. It's like a puzzle, searching for the last pieces.

You have been quoted as saying that creativity is 'not the newest sleeve; it's about finding solutions' and that 'leading the world of fashion is more important than making a beautiful garment.' Can you elaborate on this? What kind of leadership needs to happen in order to address some of the more critical issues facing fashion today?

The answer lies in the question. Leadership is needed with a critical but positive approach. Fashion is teamwork; we need to create and compose new teams.

What is the one part of the field that keeps you up at night and gets you out of bed in the morning?

I guess I feel responsible. I try to work and achieve some results. I always question myself. I don't like mediocrity. I am exigent.

You have had a multivalent, incredible career so far (Antwerp, Dries Van Noten, Polimoda...). What consumes your attention at this point in your career?

At this point of my career I feel I can choose. I can study phenomena from a distance and take time to reflect. I am very privileged to have experienced so many generations of passionate people.

What do you see your students prioritizing as their concerns? Do fashion schools and institutions have the same concerns as their students?

Fashion schools are becoming business.

Thanks Linda, Michelle

Fashion will never die. It's dominating our life and we are prisoners forever. Even when it decides to kill you, you can run but you will be unable to escape. Fashion is a strong animal eating you up like nothing in one big hug killing you slowly swallowing your blood. It's a constant fight between you and fashion, the animal, the beast. Because the beast is hungry for new food, for new ideas, for new fashion it is impossible to capture. You can once in a while escape, but then you might call yourself lucky. You might run away and hide but fashion will find you. It's like a virus, it enters your body, eats you up from the inside and then you throw it up. Once in a while you can escape by thinking of another obsession. Like work. Work is a good antidote for fashion, because it justifies your sickness. If you are obsessed by dress, you can be obsessed by work. Work is more valuable, more noble and much more useful to society. Society can easily live without fashion but not without work. So why is this hunger coming up such as a fever and is not fading away still when it is consumed? It must be a compensation of something, a drug against the emptiness of life. But maybe the beast fashion is kinder then we think, maybe it is simply to make us happy. Can we fight happiness? Of course not, we should embrace it and be even more happy to be able to have this horrible hate and love relationship with the beast. It's all a game, isn't it? A game of seduction and power; a game of hunting and be hunted. It depends what side you prefer; the hunter is equipped with technology but the beast is smarter. So either you run or you shoot the beast. But let us not dramatise the situation. The hunter is enjoying the beast on the run and the beast is thinking poor guy, I will eat him within a few minutes from now. So game goes on and meanwhile we are excited of playing a game. So please fashion, the beast, make new role models, new games so we can keep running and running and enjoying more and more of this enchantment. We are enchanted by fashion, arent't we? New rules are created in the game and of course we have to be strong again. So we start dancing with the beast, a tango, a walls, a slow, and in a strong embrace we fall in love!

The dress is traveling around the world. It encounters lovers, haters, dreamers, destroyers and provocateurs. It is a nice dress, a bit formal but not exactly boring; it has no seam, no zip and no buttons. It is a bit asymmetric and of course it's black, it smiles at you. It travelled from France to China, then to Japan and Hong Kong, landed in Dubai and finally returned to Paris. It met a friend dress, black as well, more elegant, embroidered and with a small belt. It didn't smile but had a more aggressive character. The two dresses talked a lot. They became friends. They talked about the bodies they had to dress. They were thrown on the floor, forgotten at the dry-clean shop or given away to another body. Sometimes they were in a dark cupboard for years, forgotten. It happened that the body changed, fattened and not recognisable anymore for the dress and the embarrassment was great for becoming useless. The embroidered dress said that once on a late evening she was burned! Flames destroyed her sleeve but luckily the body could repair a part of her sleeve. The nice dress had only a few compliments from admirers; the embroidered dress on the contrary had many but it seemed to her they were not very sincere. After a few years of friendship, the two dresses were separated because the two bodies travelled to different countries; one body to America and the other to India. Because of the heat the Indian body was sweating a lot and didn't wore the dress, choosing the sari which the dress could understand, while the American body was often at parties and the dress was used specially in the beginning of the body's move. Later she was forgotten and became tired and old, disrupted by time and memories, some good memories but mostly complicated memories full of extremes of joy and sorrow. Of course both dresses became out of time, démodés. This was the worst period in their lives. Why? They couldn't understand, they were upset, sad and angry! The bodies were buying others dresses less beautiful, less timeless, but they were considered modern. The bodies were restless and were buying many other dresses, given no time for adjusting a seam or a small detail to be altered. It was all so fast and they understood, no critique, they were only a dress. The bodies became older and a bit fatter and one day both bodies decided to throw their dress away. They were thrown in the green container and when they were collected they found each other back, after many travels and flights and other containers on top of each other with millions of other dresses! They fell in each other sleeves but the happiness was short. They were cut in pieces. But if you will see one day a nice carpet, black with little pieces of flowered embroideries you may step on those two dresses.

Story 3

Ai, you hurt me! Can't you use another needle? Don't take me so strongly, soften your grip. Then take the right direction, because beginning and ending has to be defined. Finally choose the right thread, the one you are using is hurting me again, it's too stiff or too thick. You need a silk thread soft, like me. I am originally from a cocoon and I came long from China thanks to a long road. I arrived here in Italy a long time ago, but I cannot remember exactly when. The road was so long and exhausting that I forgot most of the travel. We were not so many, so we felt very precious. We were thrown in a can and then they started to attack us to make us thinner to a threat; therefore, learn how to use me and how to love me without hurting me like hell! No, no, this is wrong my dear. If this is what you want use another fabric, use a nice cool wool. I know a few sheep who would be flattered to be used by you because when you put me on top of the table and I was gliding from it I immediately understood you are not an expert in using me. I am soft and I can do miracles, but I can be cold and unhappy and then it's useless to convince me to collaborate. You are wasting you time! We are not coming from the same land but we are happy to serve mankind. Do you realise how many sacrifices we had to do to make you happy? So please respect our suffering and use us well. The sheep are nice; they will not complain when you hurt them but be careful, they have a strong ego! They will be cooperative but at an ankle of a sleeve they will play you a dirty trick. They will wrinkle, like a cramp they will refuse to flatten and even hurting them with fire or heat they will make your life sound little amount of me, but if you are going to use thousands of the same of me, this will be frankly spoken a drama for you. It will make your life a misery and can be the end of your career. We need respect and we need to be admired and loved. Consider us as your friend, treat us well, nourish us well and caress us well. Ai, not against the thread... this is another mistake. I see, you are an apprentice but this does not mean you don't have to think before hurting me. Relax... Bread well, take your needle, chose the thread, put my two layers on top of each other and caress me softly. Now, kindly put your needle in my skin, again, again, again, better, mmm I start liking it, good so, you are learning fast... I feel we are becoming friends... again, again... mmmmmm...

Me at Palais de Tokyo, Paris
Drawing by Max Anish Gowriah

Me at Palais de Tokyo, Paris
Photograph by Max Anish Gowriah

Meeting a Little Boy

Paris, Palais de Tokyo
Carte Blanche to Tino Sehgal

The little boy asked me... what does progress mean for you? I said... it is not looking back, it is looking forward, like looking at a white page; you have to write new things on it; you can't copy; you can't use past ideas... you have to invent new things to write on the white page... he looked at me... he had really strong spectacles... he said... but is there something else than the white page that represents progress for you?... smart... I thought... well, yes, there are many more options, but look... we are in a white space... this is freedom, this is progress... this is a space where you can invent new things, new ideas, new expressions, new concepts... mmm... but he was fast... I saw him thinking... and he agreed, he will think later at home... strange lady... but maybe she has a point...

A young man with curled hair joined us and while walking said to me... interesting the metaphor of the white page... how do you see this as a project for the new world in progress... I said, well... we live in a globalised world, we can connect thanks to Internet... this is a new white page... I can write on my Instagram; every day is a new white page... but why are we not in peace? What is not working? Is it religion that separates us? Or is it Language... no he said, the English language now is connecting us... so, yes religion... it is how we define the concept of religion... yes, he has a point... but see there is not only language but there is also body language... In Japan I didn't spoke the language but I could connect with people thanks to accepting their body language. He was thinking... He said, I am an actor and therefore I understand.

A woman, middle aged took over... One day I had to kill my dog... my dog was sick and the veterinarian said he couldn't cure him; my dog was a substitute for my brother I lost; my father said... if you have to kill your dog you have to do it yourself! I went to the veterinarian ... but then suddenly she asked me... did you ever kill an animal? I said no... I was not a child living in the woods like you... she asked me...did you ever kill? No, no... no!...I never killed, not an animal, not a butterfly nor an insect (or maybe yes)... I don't like plants, animals... I am quite essential... I don't take care of them... they need attention and I can't give this attention... I am a product of the existential movement. She asked me... do you have pictures... no, no I have no pictures nor photographs in my living room... interesting she said...

The next woman I met, a bit younger than me, but very mature, spoke about a place where she was born; I forgot the place she mentioned but it sounded like a very far exotic place; when one day she became sick her parents sent her all alone to France, in the south... she learned to speak the language, to eat the food, to understand the people... in school she had to write with a feather, 'la plume'; she remembered one day she broke the feather; she was hardly punished; today she is a writer, but it all started when she had a computer in front of her; I understand I said; I am also writing now, only inspired my I-pad and thanks to my computer!

The next woman, my age said... I always went fishing with my father; I experienced the fish hanging on the hook and the blood that came out of the mouth of the fish. It's the first time I was confronted with death. Well, indeed as we become older death might be more in our mind, isn't it? She brought me to a wide, wide space; all people were sitting on the floor; relaxed... waiting, dreaming, resting, some walking; then suddenly a young African woman came to me; she started to tell about her grandmother, a woman with blue eyes... she was so good in story telling... she loved the mountains... she said to me... quiet! Listen to the echo, listen to the sound of the mountains. I learned so much of that woman; I was raised with white rise but I learned so much from her! Then, suddenly they all stood up making steps from left to right from behind to before; they came closer to each other intertwining, intertwining... creating tensions and then after a while of this, let's say ballet, they started running from one space to the other...

In the meantime I was attracted to a sound; it was dark... what should I do? Listen to the sound... go deeper in the dark? I hesitated... Finally, I looked to the running people from above on the stairs; a man, Indian, came to me... he asked me... where is the exhibition? The paintings? I said that's the exhibition, the people... I tried to explain, but I was so dreaming away of the experience that he maybe didn't understood; or maybe he was part of... Tino Sehgal's Carte Blanche...

HOME

'Home' means a solid shelter, a strong defence to the outside dangerous world, and a retreat from the hustle and bustle of the street. We are able to relax at home and find our sense of being, enjoying the so-called private life. 'Privacy' means what we don't want to expose, which includes physical part like our wrinkles and naked body as well as the psychological part like our sadness, fear, joy, solitude, companionship or intimacy. We can have a leisure time at home, starting a refreshing conversation with our partners or friends. Besides, it is in our own house that we keep our precious items such as portraits, our long-cherished belongings and our most beloved garments. It seems that we are strongly attached to our home. Take myself as an example. My dressing room is an important room in the house, while for my husband, it is the kitchen. The dressing room is where we keep our garments, but for me, it is more of a palace of memories. I cherish the memories of a show, a friendship, a moment of desire and a rush of excitement when I bought the garment or was wearing it. At home, I feel comfortable in my clothes, outside I try to be more formal, leaving behind my casual clothes. I want to present new silhouettes with old and new garments to become the person people know me for.

'Home' remains a place for sleep; and we have a better sleep than being in a hotel room. We enjoy the security in our blankets, our bedcovers, our cushions and we also have more space on our own bed. We can dream or work at night; we imagine having new jobs, new friends and suddenly we come up with amazing solutions to those newly emerged challenges. We have our mattresses that we care for; they give us comfort. In my neighbourhood, many mattresses are thrown away; we can catch a glimpse of them on the streets, stained and marked by an uncertain past, by passion, by love and hate. People travel, to get new jobs, and travel again to a new city where they, hopefully, will have more opportunities and therefore more success. They throw their mattresses on the streets. They are going to be happier with a new one. This is Happiness…

LESS

When 'home' is absent, people wandering on the streets will look for warmth, for survival, and eventually for some belongings. They search for what they consider indispensable for living in every quarter of the city. They pick up whatever they find valuable from carriages, shopping carts, trolleys or even trash cans where tourists and inhabitants leave their items; they collect garments, bottles, plastic bags, and anything that may contribute to their survival. In winter, they sleep on mattresses they find in the streets; in Paris, where I live now, I see many homeless people; I see them sleeping or living in fashionable districts such as Avenue Montaigne and Rue de Rivoli. They live a family life with their children lying on the streets of Paris. Some have their mobile phones with them. Probably they are refugees. But the most tender and desperate homeless people I see on the streets of Paris have few items and they have even fewer day by day. Fewer garments, less hope, less to say, less to carry, less... Covered with their dirty clothes full of stains, they hardly look at you. Not only men, but also women give up the hope. Fatalistic in their days and nights, they are confused about the time because their natural clock is disturbed by unending struggle for living. But some of them are still collecting objects, mattresses and clothes to build their own 'house'. Are those objects, gathered here or there at a special place or a special moment, becoming memories? It seems that those items are selected with due care. They finally become their property. How unbelievably tender! How unbelievably humble! Lately in Florence, I saw a homeless man accumulating paper and plastic bags from the ground, happy with whatever little piece of paper or plastic he found. This is Happiness...

Text published in the magazine *Vision*, China
Foggy Ma, Editor
September / October 2017

Expensive

When fashion is made with care it might be expensive. When it is made by hand, embroidered, cut in bias, draped and made on a specific body, it will be per definition expensive. When fashion is made in few numbers, distributed only in few specialty stores or on private on-line canals it is per definition exclusive and expensive. Especially when garments defined as a fashion item are made with a lot of attention for fabric, pattern and fit, details of buttonholes and pockets, nice collars they will be per definition expensive. The problem of expensive garments is that they are sold to wealthy people. Why is this a problem? Because wealthy people want to show that the garment they bought is expensive; the designer is trapped in overdesigning garments for a niche that maybe don't reflect society. The middle-class wealthy consumer wants also an exclusive garment but at a better price. Second lines are not the solution. Those were commercial solutions made in the 1980 for achieving a greater turnover and more visibility in advertising and editorials.

Cheap

Fashion must be cheap because we must dress billions of people. People from different origins, with different expectations and coming from different social backgrounds. People must dress for different occasions, such as work, travel, entertainment, inside the house or on the streets. In fact, there are not so many categories, but the travel category is becoming the greatest reason for being dressed. That's why shorts, t-shirts, sneakers, backpacks, jeans are the most bought garments in the world. We call this leisure wear. I call it laissez aller wear. Those who profit from this lifestyle are the e-commerce websites. They even sell saris, Qipao or cheongsam, shirts, swimwear, evening wear, chinos, sunglasses, bags, caps, t-shirts. Those items are bought on line without ever trying the garment on. If you know your size and you are familiar with a brand name you don't have to leave your house! You can buy even in the classroom listening to a boring teacher. You can spend so much on cheap garments that maybe all together what you bought in a few months is identical to one beautiful expensive garment. But that's not what you want. You want comfort, you want your tattoo visible, you want to belong to a tribe. You want to look casual! But, do you know how and where those garments are made and by whom and in which conditions? Most of you are concerned with world problems but I feel those garments are destroying a quality of life we must aspire to.

Exciting

Fashion must be exciting; when I go to a fashion show and I am not intrigued by what I see I am disappointed. It will not change my life, I will leave the location a bit lonely, with an empty feeling, like something is wrong or misunderstood, like a missed occasion, like a waste of money. The same in the store, were garments are hanging to be bought, touched or caressed. When they are not respected I feel sad. I ask myself if every person buying online or in the store is excited by what they are buying? Should we ask this question to ourselves every time we buy? Maybe yes. Let's give ourselves a mark after a shopping experience between 0 and 10. I am mostly between 7 and 10. But what if I feel guilty? Should the word guilt be introduced as a parameter for measuring consuming behaviour? For me yes, because I feel always guilty. Is guilt giving excitement? Maybe it does. Excitement returns when the shopping experience was worth it, if you feel good in the garment you bought, when it puts you in value, when you look in the mirror and say to yourself, it was a good buy, a good investment.

A Mirror of Society

Question: Does the mirror reflects the real or the unreal? Do we see ourselves in the mirror as we are or as other people see us? The difficulty of answering this question lies in the fact that nothing is real. Filming the world is filming a fake; sociologists can analyse the phenomenology of human behaviour and thus our longing for wearing black or colour. Social behaviour is traumatic and nobody is at ease in this world. We use camouflage as a pattern to make a garment strong in style, but does fashion use it as a mirror of war? Since we speak about fashion as a mark of style, reflecting the world we live in, we should believe fashion is the mirror of society. It was true in the 1960s, the 1970s, the 1980s and the 1990s; but is it still true today? Fashion is not only the mirror of the society we know the best, the one we see and experience in fashion cities such as London, Paris or Milan. It is a mirror of the new societies we accepted as being part of the fashion anxiety present in our daily life thanks to the global economy and the social or un-social media. Fashion is the mirror of this new world composed by millennium stars, by bloggers and by new faces or new values. Some are depressed because they can't find the balance between the real and the un-real and this is what we see on the catwalk. This uncertainty or unreasonable freedom of creativity is lost in chaos and depression; an atomic war is nearby and the world is shaking; cyclones are destroying the houses of millions of mostly poor people. The rich and beautiful are not really concerned and they continue to travel to fashion cities and they continue to consume. We are composed by different identities, living in different countries, doing different jobs in different time schedules and countries. This new identity is shaped by new aesthetics and new ethics.

Dark

Fashion must be dark. It is always good if there is a dark side of things whether it is a relationship, a journey, a romance, a dinner, a holiday. Travelling has always a dark side, because of delays, noisy children, waiting tiring controls, and endless waste of time and energy. But fashion is attractive if it is dark. The dark garments might show the side you are hiding and because fashion is superficial the dress or leather jacket and the boots you choose this morning might express an internal mood that you only show occasionally. Anyway, romance is so démodé and boring. We can express the sweetness of life but the darkness is more fascinating and that's what fashion should be as well. Anger can be written on t-shirts and even an artist such as Jenny Holzer is using it.

Embellishing

Embellishing is supposed to mean that fashion makes you beautiful, but the meaning of being beautiful is so differently perceived by different genders and body languages or body shapes and therefore also the messages you want to pass on to the ones who see you. The tattooed body is an embellishment that personally I have difficulty to appreciate. For the wearer of a tattooed body a t-shirt might do. If you spend a lot of money buying a nice garment you should at least feel attractive. Embellishment means that you look good. If you look good you feel good. If you feel good you catch the eye of friends, partners, and receive compliments and this makes you feel even better. Proportions of the silhouette you are going to wear must match to the proportions of your body and therefore sometimes choices are difficult to make; questions arise such as... Do I look good? Is it making me look fatter, slimmer, younger, older, shorter or is this garment me. Me in the sense how you want to be perceived. Especially young girls want to play with their sexiness, young boys with their gender, middle-aged women looking younger than their daughters and older women... well... I don't know what we are looking for. I will let you know soon.

Dramatic

Without drama fashion is flat and in most cases uninteresting. Drama gives a kind of excitement to the collections surrounded or embraced by sound, music, light or by a dramatic scenery. Drama underlines sometimes a basic way of dressing or a decadent look and feel. Both moods can be underlined adding drama as an extra flavour. Drama can be expressed thanks to a dark make-up. An intensive eye make-up gives a dramatic expression making the models protagonists of the mood of the designer. Fashion can be cruel. Designers failing to accept the stress, dying by desperation, overexposure or drugs are therefore killed by fashion and the fashion system. The performance is another interesting expression of fashion. The theatrical expression or the alienation of the world created by the designer can be more inspiring than the catwalk show where scenarios are often the same. During performances, the setting has a great impact and the dialogue within the space and the viewer. The 'tableau vivant' is a great tool for transmitting the look and feel of a collection. Film is a great inspiration for many designers and artists like David Lynch's drama inspired many.

Romantic

Life is less and less romantic. Life is more and more cruel. Therefore, we can create a dream world thanks to clothes, long evening dresses, fringes, embroidery, transparency. Escapism is an easy tool for fashion to forget the world outside, the world full of fear and uncertainties. Embroidery and beautiful wedding dresses are capable to overrule the drama of today's events. They can blind us for a while and make us think we are happy. Iconic romantic pieces can be made in 3D such as the master Iris van Herpen is masterly doing. Her handcraft translated in new technology is creating a new romantic atmosphere. The exhibition *Manus x Machina* at the Metropolitan Museum in New York in 2017, curated by Andrew Bolton, was a great example of beauty and technical skills. Romance is cruel and can kill love. The love and hate relationship within fashion has a decadent connotation. It is therefore important to have both approaches in our work, whether it is design, communication, education or just the act of buying. The tension created by this duality is resulting in romance. The theatrical and the drama are embracing each other and create fashion within a romantic expression. Mozart is the perfect example of crazy romance ending in complete folly touching the borders of insanity.

Successful

A designer must be successful; an artist must be successful. Success can be measured by the turnover of the business. It can be measured by the quantity or the quality of shops or the gallery owners or the curators and art lovers who appreciate your work. It happens that artist or designers are happy without economic success. This is perfect for their private satisfaction, they enjoy life as it is, without complexes or traumas. The business of art and fashion is not interested in this happiness... no time to waste. Success can be achieved by the personality of the artist, by its originality or by the absolute stubbornness, that at the end of the road, is winning the confidence of its audience and become a star.

Sharp

Fashion needs clear messages. Sharpness is the easiest way for the de-

...igner to express its state of mind. My advice has always been the following: Be sharp, be essential, be to the point, clarify your silhouette, we have no time to listen to long stories or endless explanations. Sharpness means not too many fringes, simplicity is key. Use fringes but use them well. When the silhouette is overloaded by too many ideas chaos takes over. Don't overact; your customer is not stupid, he or she will buy your garment if it is attractive. Sharpness is a little secret that when used well might become a signature.

Inspired

Inspiration is the start of a new collection, or maybe it can be boredom as well. Boredom can inspire but also a nice sunset can or a bunch of flowers. Inspiration is unpredictable, it can bring your mind in a state of ecstasy o give your heart a boom... Sorrow and joy can inspire as pain or pleasure can do. The balance between the inspirational moment and the practice is the moodboard though. When the team around the table starts working on the collection, the moodboard, the imagery must inspire others. When a collection is inspired, the audience such as the buyers, press, friends critics can feel the energy of the inspired moments where the collection is based upon. Inspiration might sometimes overrule the collection. The designer is panicking about the lack of time, about a negative comment on the previous collection or simply because she/he is not inspired. When later the photographer or stylist take one garment out of the collection they should feel inspiration thru the textile, the colour, the shape, the seam, the collar, the sleeve. Here we recognise real creativity!

Embraced

If we embrace fashion, it will embrace you. Embracing fashion is also embracing its changing attitudes, its uncertainties, its debates, its controversies, its problems, its love and hate moods, its ingratitudes, its tiring waitings at shows, or its attractive attire. Embracing fashion is embracing the hard work it requires. Its high rhythm of performance. Embracing fashion is accepting to feel captured in its charm, taking the risk to be rejected...

Superficial

Today fashion must be superficial as we are living at a fast pace; if we go deep at wearing or designing a garment we need time; can you imagine that we are going to our tailor to make a dress or a suit that will need six or seven 'rendezvous' chatting with friends while drinking a glass of champagne? And if the dress is made on a body that is not of a perfect fit more time is needed, more fitting, more afternoons of enjoyment, not forgetting the hours we dedicate for choosing the fabric, the colour, the embellishments, the shoe, the bag. Today we order a dress by clicking on the computer and it will be delivered in one or two days. It seems to me we are offered more superficially designed dresses for doing this activity. Superficiality is not always synonym of fastness, but in many cases it is. We buy a shoe in thirty minutes or even less. We know our label and when we put them on at home in our dressing room the shoes are joining other shoes we bought in the past.

Entertainment

Many fashion shows are not simply shows where models walk on a cat-walk. It is an event planned carefully by a team of hundreds of people. Resort collections are shown in places like the Sahara, in Japan... or on the top of a hill. Paris, the capital of fashion, is specialised in great scenography and I think of the Dior shows I had the opportunity to attend. Some shows are emotionally so strong that tears are flowing; I am special-ly thinking of Dries Van Noten's fashion shows. Some are performances and I remember those of Bernhard Willhelm or of Martin Margiela's early days. Locations are remote and to arrive at the venue is a challenge for many. Press is of course privileged by special cars and private drivers, but for buyers and observers it is a real voyage. Before and after the show the kisses of friends, journalists and buyers are kisses to old friends sounding like a family reunion. Fashion is entertainment and the consumer is not always part of those exciting moments.

Economically Viable

If a brand is conceptually interesting but the sales are poor, the cash flow situation will become problematic; the brand has to find an investor or will stop its activities after a three-year period. A financial plan will be made if this is missing or incomplete and a collection plan with more commercial by adding items that will sell. No escape is possible! Price settings are of great importance not to lose money by making prototypes; in many cases starting designers are surrounded by friends who support the start of the brand. Later specialists are entering the company to make the brand more profitable. Those elements are a natural evolution in fashion companies and not problematic; only fast and efficient decisions can save a good brand from disappointments.

Personal

If the designer fails he/she fails because he/she is lacking a personal vision; if vision is equal to style he/she is in big trouble. Personality is important as identity is. Both are linked because personality is created by a personal attitude. Collections, especially in the middle segment, are often lacking a personal touch. Designers can improve or learn to have a personal vision. Good fashion education is helping them to develop their identity. Not only the collection has to be immediately recognised and has to have hanger appeal but the imagery, the logo or non-logo, the photography, the advertising must be in balance with the brand. The concepts of being personal and having a personality are overlapping. Many designers are lacking personality and are therefore overruled by the system; maybe they are good but they lack long-term vision.

Made of Great Quality Fabrics

Fabrics are the key element of a good collection. If fabrics are of second- or third-rate quality design will never have a luxury feel. The consumer is unaware of this detail but sometimes he or she recognises the problem instinctively. Fabrics can destroy or make a garment. Finish, cut, patterns are also part of the game and the conspiracy, but fabrics are playing an important role in the final success. If you pay your garment a good price the fabric is super important; if you pay less or you pay little money you are more tolerant towards the longevity of the fabric and the garment. The fabric resists to your body language or activities, to your sweat or to your care or un-care, to your dry-cleaner or to your washing machine. Why are some designer labels expensive? Because they create, design their own fabrics in exclusivity. Important is to recognise the hand of the designer regarding his choice of fabrics.

Based on Passion
Without passion fashion is uninteresting. To work in fashion and to build a career, passion is the main element and the key for success.

Fashion must be... created not designed

Fashion must be... produced

Fashion must be... distributed

Fashion must be... loved

Fashion must be... hated

Fashion must be... a container of ideas

Fashion must be... modern

Fashion must be...

WE WALKED IN THE WORLD / WE WERE MANY / WE WALKED IN
THE PARK / THERE WAS SILENCE / WE WALKED ON THE BEACH /
THERE WAS SOUND AND LIGHT / WE WALKED IN THE MOUNTAINS /
THERE WAS HAPPINESS / WE WALKED IN CITIES / THERE WAS
ENERGY / WE WALKED / WE ARE HAPPY...

AS LONG AS THE SUN SHINES ON THE MOON / AS LONG AS THE
EARTH GIVES SHADOW TO THE MOON / AS LONG AS WE ARE THE
UNIVERSE / WE ARE MULTIVERSE / AS LONG AS / WE ARE...

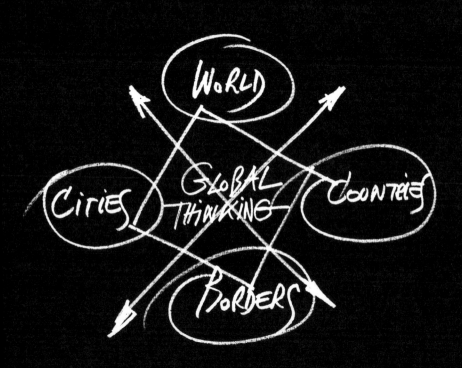

Conversation

Anna Yudina: I suggest talking about some of the more ambiguous, more subtle aspects that keep coming up throughout your book. Things like chaos and vulnerability; anger and solitude; making mistakes and experiencing loneliness; and also taking your time and using your intuition. We seek to avoid most of them and are unsure of how to deal with some others, but it's crucial to recognise their value, which I think you did. Seen from the *core-of-the-vortex* perspective, they become an integral part of the creative process... *Chaos* would be a good starting point for this conversation.

Linda Loppa: We feel that the society is a bit upside down today. There is no single style or movement that precisely reflects today's state of mind. No vision coming from the people who are our icons; the icons are not saying clearly what they stand for. Be it in politics or culture, food or literature, there is great freedom that creates chaos. On one hand, it's positive because everything is possible, but on the other hand, uncertainty scares a lot of people. I always see the positive side of it because I'm not living in the past. There are values like integrity or the ability to express yourself that should still be respected, but we should also embrace the freedom that we have today and try to see it as a personal challenge. It feels like 1968, when people were getting out on the streets and there were new ways to look at things. It's a moment to jump into this chaos and find your solutions. To try and bring to your field what you think is important. Breakthroughs always happen in times of chaos. Renaissance, too, was a chaotic period.

'Chaos' has a connotation of being lost, but that's not true. You can organise chaos. You can define it as a diagram that contains all the possible problems and all the possible solutions, and map out the possible collaborations between the people in this chaotic society. What we are doing is mapping. Maybe mapping is one of the new ways to organise education as well.

AY: One particular moment where chaos massively enters into the picture is making a career choice. We are no longer satisfied with conventional job descriptions. The definition of creative professions evolves; design coexists and cooperates with other practices and fields of knowledge. Navigating this sea of yet-to-be-defined potentials where excitement blends with uncertainty is exactly what you've called 'entering the chaos'.

LL: I myself am a perfect example! I have been studying Latin and Greek and, although I enjoyed the subject, I didn't like the mentality of the teachers at the time, so I jumped into the Academy of Fine Arts. There I was my own self, surrounded by creativity. The freedom of creative education was key to the successes of the people we know today. Education should become less rigid and — using this fashionable word — more 'hybrid', multidisciplinary, so that, while studying, we could get in touch with more of different fields and open our mind. If you specialise from the start, you learn more and more about less and less, until finally you know everything about nothing. But the more you train your brain to embrace chaos, the more your mind becomes open and flexible, the better it absorbs innovation. Instead of always referring to ourselves and to our past, we need more exchange. Then we will be more open to other cultures, other ways of thinking, other methods of working, and will be able to understand each other better.

Understanding others is the priority. By doing so, you can also understand what you don't want to be. Sometimes you discover yourself by eliminating all that doesn't feel like you until you find something that feels right. There are different ways to arrive to your identity, but it takes time and is composed of different layers of experience. Every layer is important, even a mistake in your strategy can tell you something about yourself. The society today must allow failure. That's why I think that chaos is good — because it leads to a more open mind-set.

In fashion, that freedom has created an enormous shift in aesthetics. I often have to remind myself to not judge negatively the things that I don't like. Today, I have to analyse more carefully what's behind the collection — the context, the message, the designer's personality, and what he or she wants to achieve. The parameters are broader now. Once I could say it was a beautiful collection'. I can't say this anymore. This doesn't mean you can't have an opinion, but, before you form an opinion, you have more steps to take. I sometimes see the same collection three-four times to understand it better.

AY: What questions do you ask yourself when seeing a collection?

LL: Aesthetically speaking, I have to be careful not to judge too fast. But my ethics hasn't changed. I can feel if a designer is being honest or if they are playing a game. I have experience, knowledge and intuition to see if they have a long-term vision or if their collection is a tryout, a test. You have to read through the image; to analyse what kind of psychology is going on behind the scenes. I can make mistakes, but most often my feeling is correct.

AY: Here is another keyword: *intuition*. Immensely valuable but almost equally elusive when we are trying to pin it down. This inner voice we hear when should we acknowledge it as the intuition that can be trusted? Can one learn to be more intuitive?

LL: As a child, intuition is something you can access immediately. You are born with it. I'm not sure if there is a method to fully understand intuition but I think that you can train it by deduction and by analysing your behaviour. For a leader of a team that I've always been, intuition is really important. Defining what we are going to work on, understanding what we are having in front of us as a problem requires intuition. There's also empathy, of course. And the third element is knowledge, the need to analyse the situation, to break it into short- and long-term planning. They call it management, although I'm not sure if management courses are based on intuition. But it's not by taking a management course that you become a good manager. If you want to be a good manager, you need an intuitive understanding of the direction in which you want to develop

AY: This involves *risk-taking*. Doing your best and dealing with the fear of *mistakes* and *failures*.

LL: Taking risks is certainly a jump into the void. As a leader, you need to take risks, and sometimes you won't sleep at night. It's your intuition that gives you the strength to take risks. The only thing is that if you make a mistake as a leader of your team, you divide that mistake with a lot of people. That's something I always try to avoid. In your personal life, you just take the consequences of your risks, and that's probably the exciting part, the life's pepper and salt.

AY: It's also about accepting your *vulnerability*. Aren't young creatives especially vulnerable because they are putting themselves and their ideas out there for the first time — and have to face all kinds of critique, both constructive and mean, and learn to move on?

LL: I see it differently. When you are younger, you can hide your fragility, but as you grow older, it becomes more visible. Your challenges become more complex. You feel the fear of falling behind. And, while your experience allows you to see solutions more clearly, bringing them into practice within today's chaotic situation can be more difficult.

I feel more vulnerable today. The sense that your time is running short makes you feel fragile. You are happy with what you have achieved, and you have the luggage to draw your knowledge from, but there is also uncertainty about what you are going to achieve next.

AY: Which brings us to *taking time.* Today, more than ever, we feel that, if we don't want to fall behind, we have to think, act, learn and adapt very fast. How does the ability to take your time become vital in this environment?

LL: I love the fastness of today because it gives me the push that I need not to feel vulnerable. It stimulates me. But if you have to develop a strategy for a long term vision, you still need time for making the best choice. To find the answer, you need that time when your mind is empty, when time stands still.

AY: Are you saying that you need this high-speed, high-pressure reality in order to intensify your thinking, but then you need a moment of stillness to allow for the solution to come?

LL: Yes. It's always good to have the pressure of deadlines, of meetings and challenges. And then you are sitting on a beach and dreaming away, or drinking your tea, or reading a book, or looking at the stars, or sleeping — and that phrase suddenly comes to you! It has happened to me so many times: you are looking for something while you are being fast, but there is no room for it. Then you slow down, and suddenly the solution is there!

AY: Carving out space for *nothingness*…

LL: Nothingness — which we now have less and less of. iPhone is a fantastic way to connect with people or share things, but I'm not sure if constantly having iPhones in our hands — me, too! — is not a handicap for creating those timeless moments.
More and more often I'm having students come to me without their smartphones and computers, just to have a conversation, and I appreciate this incredibly. Both of us stay completely open-minded, chatting about whatever, and suddenly you recognise them as a person. You have tears in your eyes when this happens!

AY: These 'timeless moments of stillness' rhyme with the need for solitude. You speak about *loneliness* and *solitude* more than once throughout the book.

LL: To me, this is not a sad thing. As young people, we were all dreamers. You don't want to be like the others. Loneliness is an attitude of saying 'I'm different, I'm not like you.' In a way, you create your loneliness to be different — but then you need your solitude to make decisions and to actually prove that you are different.

AY: You also confess that you are at your best when feeling angry, frustrated, not accepting the status quo. How does one use *anger* productively?

LL: When people step on my toes, or when I'm angry about something, it feels like adrenaline rush. It stimulates my thinking; it lights my fire. It's like a bomb of energy.

AY: There are other moments though, when jumping in should take turns with stepping out and becoming an observer.

LL: When you step out of the circle of ideas and society, you observe, you screen your environment; you know immediately why you have stepped out and how you can re-enter.

Florence, 12 March 2019

Acknowledgements

I dedicate this book to all the people I mentioned in it; they inspired me to start writing. I want to thank all my colleagues with whom I worked in those many years; first those of the Royal Academy Fashion Department, secondly my colleagues of my second important team, the one of MoMu museum in Antwerp, and finally those I worked with the last thirteen years, the Polimoda team; I want to thank especially Danilo Venturi who inspired me inventing a new language and pushed me for publishing this book. I have to thank the many friends I made in fashion all over the world, and the people I worked with making exhibitions in Antwerp and in Florence. I must thank all the people who followed me in many of my crazy adventures related to education, to museum management and curating and who are going to follow me and support me in all the projects I am planning for the future. My greatest thanks go to all the artists whom I followed during their careers as they were so important to the person I am today. I have to thank Fashion as a whole; you are my family and without you I would not be the person I am. Thanks to the many students and designers I encountered and for the many conversations we had; they are part of the memories needed to embrace the future. Thanks to Florence; the city and the people living and working to create a renewed energy that I feel on my skin, a city me and my husband call now home.

Finally, I need to thank Eve Leckey who during the many years I was writing, corrected my first drafts and commented on the content, giving me the courage to continue writing. Thanks to Bradley Quinn for having organised a meeting with Maria, mother of Anna Yudina whom I met in Paris only recently. Anna helped me through the book with her strength and advice giving me the confidence I needed to re-start working with renewed passion on the final chapter of *Life is a Vortex*.

Thanks to Skira and Polimoda for publishing the book.

Thanks to all the persons I didn't mention but who are in my mind and soul.

Linda Loppa
5 April 2019

Editing
Anna Albano

Graphic design
Open Lab

First published in Italy in 2019 by

Skira editore S.p.A.
Palazzo Casati Stampa
via Torino 61, 20123 Milano, Italy
www.skira.net

Printed and bound in Italy. First edition

ISBN: 978-88-572-4062-6

Distributed in USA, Canada, Central & South
America by ARTBOOK | D.A.P. 75, Broad Street
Suite 630, New York, NY 10004, USA.
Distributed elsewhere in the world by Thames
and Hudson Ltd., 181A High Holborn, London
WC1V 7QX, United Kingdom.